Margaret Chase Smith

WOMAN OF COURAGE

Books by Frank Graham, Jr.

MARGARET CHASE SMITH—*Woman of Courage*

IT TAKES HEART (*with Mel Allen*)

CASEY STENGEL: *His Half-Century in Baseball*

Margaret Chase Smith

WOMAN OF COURAGE

by FRANK GRAHAM, Jr.

THE JOHN DAY COMPANY : *New York*

*Library of Congress Catalogue
Card Number: 64-15625*

MANUFACTURED IN THE UNITED STATES OF AMERICA

PREFACE

This book is not intended to be a formal biography of Margaret Chase Smith. It is, rather, designed to describe the professional life of a United States Senator. The author might have chosen as his subject any of the other ninety-nine members of the Senate. He settled on Senator Margaret Chase Smith not only because she is one of the most able, independent and respected members of that body, but because the special problems she has encountered there as a woman add both spice to the story and significance to the record.

Though he consulted a great many books while putting this one together, the author is especially indebted to the following books and *their* authors:

Congress and the American Tradition by James Burnham. Henry Regnery Company, Chicago, 1959.

Politics U.S.A. James M. Cannon, Editor. Doubleday & Company, Garden City, New York, 1960.

5

Congress—Its Contemporary Role by Ernest S. Griffith. New York University Press, 1956.

U.S. Senators and Their World by Donald R. Matthews. The University of North Carolina Press, Chapel Hill, 1960.

Ladies of Courage by Eleanor Roosevelt and Lorena Hickok. G. P. Putnam's Sons, New York, 1954.

The Lady and the Vote by Marion Sanders. The Riverside Press, Cambridge, 1956.

Citadel: The Story of the U.S. Senate by William S. White. Harper & Bros., New York, 1956.

The following publications were sources of some of the material in this book: *The Saturday Evening Post, This Week, The New Republic, Time, The Nation, Down East, The New York Times,* the New York *Herald Tribune,* the New York *Post, The Christian Science Monitor,* the Washington *Post,* the Portland *Press-Herald* and the Bangor *Daily News.*

Articles by the following writers were especially helpful to this author: Marquis Childs, May Craig, Doris Fleeson, Richard Hallet, Murray Kempton, Ruth Montgomery, Drew Pearson, Josephine Ripley, Courtney Sheldon, Beverly Smith, Richard L. Strout and David Wise.

The author also wishes to thank Ben Harding of Rockland, Maine, Henry Gosselin of the Somerset *Reporter* and Mary Marston of the Skowhegan Public Library for the time they generously gave him; and Mrs. Ellen Strout of Milbridge, Maine, for her help in typing the manuscript.

Margaret Chase Smith

WOMAN OF COURAGE

Illustrations follow page 128.

～ 1 ～

ALL day Monday she could be seen moving across the floor of the Senate Chamber, a slender woman with neat white hair and a brisk step. Occasionally she stopped to talk to men whose names and faces were familiar to millions of Americans; more often she listened intently as these men, her colleagues, spoke. Then she passed on again . . . saying a few words, asking a question, listening.

It was September 23, 1963. At ten-thirty the next morning the United States Senate would convene to carry out one of its most important and treasured functions. The Limited Test Ban Treaty, which diplomats of the United States, Great Britain and the Soviet Union had recently hammered out in Moscow, and which outlawed nuclear explosions in the atmosphere, water and outer space, was to come before the Senate to be ratified or rejected. There was no doubt about the outcome of the vote. More than the necessary two-thirds of the Senate's members had agreed to approve the treaty. Among the tiny handful who had not yet made up their minds was the senior Senator from Maine, Margaret Chase Smith.

"It will be perhaps the most difficult vote of my career," she told reporters. "I just don't know how I will vote. I don't know."

Throughout the day dozens of newspapermen, and representatives of radio and television, pressed her for an answer. The mail which lay on her desk in the New Senate Office Building reflected this national concern over her final decision: some of it was from Maine, but much more of it was from elsewhere in the country. She had received almost ten thousand letters on the subject. This mail ran, she said, eight to one against the treaty's ratification, but it would not sway her vote.

"I shall cast my vote on the basis of the best judgment I have on the merits of the issue," she said, "on the basis of as much information as I have been able to obtain, on the logical answers to my questions, and not on the emotions of extremists."

She recorded a statement for her constituents, to be played that evening over radio stations in Maine. While the treaty was certain to be ratified, she said, it would not reflect the "real attitude" of the Senate.

"Make no mistake about it," she told her listeners, "the misgivings about the treaty are many and are deep. Many, many Senators will vote for it who are doing so with great reluctance and with great fear that they are making a mistake. I, for one, will feel that whichever way I vote will in the future prove to be a tragic mistake."

It was a feverish, tiring day on the Senate floor. Time and again the bell rang to summon members for a roll call vote. Amendments to the treaty were proposed. One by one they were considered and rejected. When Margaret Smith voted against an amendment which had been proposed by Senator Barry Goldwater, observers in the press gallery thought they had found a clue to how she would vote on the treaty itself. Their reasoning seemed logical: earlier it had been rumored that Margaret Smith, anxious to run for Vice-President of the United States on a Goldwater ticket in 1964, would line up with him on this vote. When she didn't, it was assumed that the rumors of her attempt to please Goldwater were untrue, and that she would vote the next day for the treaty's ratification, which Goldwater already had promised to vote against.

Between roll calls, Margaret Smith listened to the speeches, asked questions privately of other members, and kept her own counsel. Though besieged by reporters for her decision, she was not under pressure from her colleagues. They were anxious to discuss the treaty with her, but no one tried to sway her vote.

Strength, embodied in a man or a woman, always draws respectful attention. In the Senate this day, strength was manifested in the person of a Richard Russell of Georgia, a Hubert Humphrey of Minnesota, an Everett Dirksen of Illinois, a Barry Goldwater of Arizona. It was the strength of men who deal in power drawn from the blocs of other men they lead. Margaret Smith's strength has a lonelier, more personal source. Independent (according to her friends) or stubborn (according to her enemies), she has remained aloof from the orthodox political structure and stances which might have won her a large following among professional politicians. The Republicans count her in their party, but no party can count on her vote.

Cool and feminine in this overwhelmingly masculine assembly, Margaret Smith would have been, in any case, an object of admiration. Well-tailored, with a fondness for a fragile rose or a simple necklace, she would naturally be deferred to by those male Senators for whom gallantry is a cherished ritual of their tradition-haunted chamber. A woman of sixty-five, poised and contained, with a hint of severity in her dry Yankee voice, she would command respect in any gathering by her physical presence alone. Yet it was more even than the sum of these qualities which caused national attention to be focused on her in this dramatic hour. Margaret Smith is driven by a devotion to public life more often associated with distant and spartan ages than with our own flabbier, complex time. Her final decision would be, not a reaction to public or party pressure, but the product of her years in public life.

The debate continued on the floor of the Senate. It was stimulated, in great part, by Margaret Smith. She had posed a total of sixteen "basic and troubling" questions, for which she hoped to get answers from President John F. Kennedy and his military advisers. Behind the questions was Margaret Smith's uneasiness about whether the treaty would undermine America's national security. Are we able to detect all nuclear detonations occurring in the three environments specified by the treaty? Will the treaty keep us from ever developing and using any defense against missile attacks? Will the treaty enable the Russians to equal the effectiveness of our low-yield tactical weapons while preventing us from catching up with them in the high-yield race?

"Without satisfactory answers to these and other questions," she said, "it will be virtually impossible for any of us to measure and evaluate the gains versus the risks of entering into this limited test ban treaty."

These searching questions formed the bedrock of the Senate debate. President Kennedy tried to answer some of them on a nationally televised program. Secretary of State Dean Rusk and Secretary of Defense Robert S. McNamara tried to answer others. Senator John Sparkman of Alabama devoted an entire speech to Margaret Smith's questions on the floor of the Senate. In an impassioned speech there, Rhode Island's Senator John O. Pastore assured his colleagues that the United States was not negotiating with Russia from a position of weakness. Like the President, he urged them to vote for the treaty.

On Tuesday morning, September 24, ninety-nine Senators

(the hundredth, Clair Engle, lay ill in a California hospital) assembled in the Capitol for the historic vote. In the minds of many lay memories of the Senate vote which had killed Woodrow Wilson's plan to bring our country into the League of Nations after World War One. The Senate's aversion to foreign entanglements then had helped to create the conditions which brought on World War Two. That time, as Columnist James Reston phrased it, the Senate "bet on its fears . . . so this time it bet on its hopes."

This was a solemn occasion. Many Senators shared Margaret Smith's uneasiness about the treaty, but had resolved to vote for it. President Kennedy, calling it the first tiny step toward genuine peace, had said that the treaty "carried the hopes of the world." Aware of the profound importance of their action that morning, the assembled Senators broke a long-standing tradition: they allowed themselves to be photographed in a group, sitting at their desks in the Senate Chamber.

The roll call began. It was clear that each Senator was voting as he had announced he would. The "ayes" piled up vote after vote for the treaty. Margaret Smith's name was called.

"No," she answered. Her voice carried distinctly through the chamber, unlike her usual half-muted responses. It caused the only stir that morning in the Senate.

After the treaty had been ratified by a vote of 80–19, newsmen questioned Margaret Smith about her vote. Replying that she had cast "a very troubled vote" against the treaty, she went on to say:

"I have very grave misgivings about the harmful effects of rejection of the treaty. But in my opinion the jeopardy that the treaty imposes on our national security is a more compelling reason for its rejection than the political and psychological disadvantages that would stem from rejection of the treaty."

Her vote had gone against her party (most Republicans voted for the treaty) and against the country's progressive elements with which she had often sided in the past. It had gone against the passionate desire of many American men and women to call a halt to the frightening nuclear arms race, and the atmospheric poisons which were the residue of frequent nuclear testing. Those people who know her best rejected any attempt to ascribe her negative vote to her personal ambitions. It was a vote, right or wrong, popular or unpopular, based on a profound conviction. If it can be explained at all, that explanation will be found in the special experience of this remarkable politician.

～ 2 ～

MARGARET SMITH, when she worked for her hometown newspaper, advanced the cause of its advertising and circulation departments by plugging the slogan: "There are eleven Bostons, many Londons, but only one Skowhegan." No one has ever contradicted her on that point.

Had she been searching for comparisons rather than distinctions she might have mentioned that Skowhegan, like Paris and New York, sprang up on a river island, overflowed to the mainland and took its place in history. The Kennebec is the river on which Skowhegan stands, in west-central Maine, and which served as the mainstream of its early life. There are falls at this point in the Kennebec. There, before the coming of the white settlers, Kennebec Indians came to fish for salmon, and the town's name, Skowhegan, is an Indian word meaning "The Place to Watch": the place to watch for fish.

History and the white man arrived in the area at the end of the seventeenth century. Father Sebastien Rasles, a French Jesuit priest, came to work with the Indians; he was killed during a British raid on his settlement. The first English colonists built their homes on "Skowhegan Island" in 1771. Past this spot, in 1775, General Benedict Arnold led his ragged army along the banks of the Kennebec on his way to the unsuccessful siege of Quebec; a granite boulder on the island commemorates that march today, while musket balls and other reminders of the march have been picked up along the river's banks.

Skowhegan (it took that name in 1836) grew and prospered during the nineteenth century. All year round it took its nourishment from the broad blue river that, for its people, is more than a constant presence. The Kennebec flows out of Moosehead Lake to the north, winds through the Maine forests and past the little shore towns for 150 miles, and finally mingles with the waters of the Atlantic at the port of Bath. In summer the lumbermen floated their logs down the river to the mills below Skowhegan, each four-foot log bearing the color mark of the mill for which it was destined, the wood clogging along the shore at the bend beyond the town and then fanning out in the great eddy which is today a tourist sight.

In winter the river bore an even more colorful pageant. When the mercury dipped below freezing,

> And birds sit brooding in the snow,
> And Marion's nose looks red and raw,

the men and the boys of the Kennebec region took out and sharpened their cutting tools and converged on the river where the blue flowing waters of summer had hardened into steel-blue ice. Dressed against the cold in their bright caps and woolen jackets, the workers carved the river's ice into great cubes. Then laboring, steaming horses dragged the frozen harvest to nearby icehouses, where it was piled until spring. When the river had melted and the waters ran free again, sturdy, four-masted sailing ships came slowly up the river, towed by tugs, and the men of the towns slid the heavy chunks of ice into the wide holds. And then the ships were off again, down the river and into the Atlantic and away to distant ports, and the food and drink of half the world was chilled by Kennebec ice.

It was into this frozen world that Margaret Madeline Chase was born on December 14, 1897. If there was prosperity in Skowhegan then, the Chase family did not share in it. They had, at one time. Her great-grandfather had owned land south of Skowhegan, and her grandfather, John Wesley Chase, had fought in the Civil War before returning to Skowhegan to become a Methodist minister.

Her father had not prospered. The prospects of George Chase, a balding, round-faced man, had seemed bright enough early in life. But blinding headaches afflicted him. He courted, and finally married in 1896, the daughter of a worker in the local sash and blind factory. Her name was Carrie Murray. In their six children was to mingle George's Irish-English blood, and Carrie's Scotch and French-Canadian blood. Margaret was the eldest of their children; two boys died young, while another, Wilbur, has lived all his life in Skowhegan and now works in the local State Liquor Store. There were two other girls, Laura (now Laura Bernier of Chevy Chase, Maryland) and Evelyn (now Evelyn St. Ledger of Skowhegan).

After their marriage, George and Carrie Chase settled on North Avenue in the five-room, white frame house which her father had built with his own hands. Though George worked as a headwaiter in the Coburn Hotel when times were especially hard, he was known in Skowhegan as a barber. His shop was next to his home. There, in the afternoons, little Margaret would walk into the curious shop, where the talk was man's talk, where each customer had his squat shaving mug on the crowded shelf and the entire scene was recreated in the long, gilt-edged mirror which ran almost the length of a side wall. The room was immaculate, and Margaret came to know the unique spicy smells of a nineteenth-century barbershop. George Chase charged the standard price for a haircut—fifteen cents. It really wasn't much of a living, even in those days, for a man with four growing children.

"We certainly didn't go hungry," Margaret Smith has said in later years, "but we didn't have anything."

Her mother kept the family together, providing a clean home and going to work outside when there was less money than usual. She took many different jobs, each of them for a short time: working in the five-and-ten, or the shoe factory, or in the Coburn Hotel as a waitress. "Mother was a great believer in the home," Margaret Smith says. "She saw to it that we always lived together as a family."

Margaret Smith remembers the struggle and the planning that kept the family together. "Mother always got my clothes too big so I could grow into them," she says. It was embarrassing sometimes for this proud young girl, but she accepted it as she accepted all the other aspects of life in Skowhegan. There wasn't time to brood about what she didn't have. "Mother always felt that if she kept us busy we'd be the better for it," and young Margaret learned early how to help in the kitchen, making blueberry muffins, clam chowders and baked beans. It has been written that Margaret, when the barbershop was crowded, also took her turn at clipping the customer's hair; this she denies.

But George and Carrie Chase did not neglect the other part of their children's life. Mrs. Chase bought a piano for them and paid fifty cents apiece for Margaret's lessons. And every holiday was noted with the appropriate ceremonies.

"We were always taught to do things for ourselves," Margaret Smith has said. "Mother would bring home tissue paper and we'd make our own May baskets. On Memorial Day we'd go out in the woods and get violets and cherry blossoms for wreaths to put on the graves. And at Christmas we always went out in the country in the wagon and got our own spruce tree. We made our own decorations with popcorn and cranberries and we'd fill those little green cloth bags full of oranges. We made a lot over things like that. Our Christmas presents were always things we were going to get anyway."

And, in keeping with Carrie Chase's belief that the family must stay together, she encouraged her children to have their parties at home. If it happened to be the birthday of one of them, she would arrange a party for her own and the neighborhood children, and George Chase would make ice cream, sometimes flavored with field strawberries, in the old-fashioned hand freezer set on the back stoop. The Chase children, of course, knew how to entertain themselves. Margaret played the piano at their parties, and they organized amateur theatricals, tacking butcher paper to the barn walls for painted scenery.

But what they looked forward to most of all were the outdoor excursions of summer. The area around Skowhegan, with its rolling hills and cool, clear lakes, is one of the loveliest in Maine. The children fidgeted through the long Saturday afternoons, while George Chase shaved and cut the hair of the country customers who crowded his shop to be dandied up for the weekend. The men swapped tales, or commented in pungent phrases on people whose names were brought up ("He'll shave you close," they'd say of an old Yankee trader, "but he won't hack you," and everybody would get a laugh out of that).

Carrie Chase and the children would have packed the picnic baskets and the warm clothes (for there is a chill in Maine nights, even in the middle of summer) long before George Chase cut the last head of hair and closed up his shop for the weekend. There would be sandwiches and homemade cookies and a jug of lemonade; chunks of ice, wrapped in grain bags, would chill the lemonade when they were ready to drink it. And then they would all climb into his buckboard, pulled by the team of strong horses George Chase kept in the barn behind the maple-shaded house, and set off for a weekend of adventure.

"We'd drive out to Smithfield Pond, which was one of the Belgrade lakes," Margaret Smith says. "It was a long way and so we'd always get there late Saturday night. But at three-thirty Dad would be up dragging somebody out of bed to go fishing with him, and he'd usually get me because I'd be the only one who would go with him. By four we'd be out in a boat trolling for white perch."

Cabins at Smithfield Pond cost a dollar a day. It was a lot for the Chases, but they made the trip as often as they were able during Maine's short summer. "It was about the only thing other than necessities the family spent their money on," Margaret Smith recalls. "We'd have wonderful times out there. They had lovely beaches and the water wasn't too cold. I can remember how we used to ride the horses into the lake."

But Margaret had a life of her own too. At twelve she decided to supplement the family income. She applied for a job at the Green Brothers' five-and-ten where her mother had often worked, but the store apparently wasn't quite ready for her.

"We'll hire you, sure," the manager said. "But you have to be able to reach the shelves."

Margaret couldn't quite make it. When she was thirteen she returned and was promptly hired; she could reach the shelves, though she had to stand on a box for the high ones. Her pay was ten cents an hour. On Saturday nights, when the weather was too cold for an excursion to Smithfield Pond, she would work five hours for fifty cents.

She was making progress in school, too. In high school, where she took a commercial course, she was a hard-working student who earned the respect of her teachers and classmates. Her English teacher, Dorothy Elliott, was to say of her in 1948: "At seventeen she was exactly the same person she is today. Her essential qualities have matured. They haven't changed." She was interested in everything; she went out for the school basketball team, and helped it to win the state championship in her senior year. Outfitted in a middy blouse and black bloomers, she was the team's side center and manager.

As graduation day at Skowhegan High School approached in 1916, Margaret Chase was already an imposing young woman: confident and competent, she was also handsome, with dark hair and prominent yet pleasing features, and remarkable eyes which were clear and blue in repose, and positively frosty in moments of stress and anger. Her work in the five-and-ten store had been valuable in at least one respect. The skimpy wages she had received left her with a quick sympathy for the workingman, which has been reflected in her liberal labor record in Congress. She also followed her mother and father by working at the Hotel Coburn. For a while she waited on tables, and afterward she ran the hotel's telephone switchboard ("In a small town the telephone operator knew everything and everybody and was considered an important person") and she was sometimes paid as much as a dollar for a single night's work.

Still, there were moments of diversion. Often at night there was a call to the switchboard from Skowhegan's First Selectman, Clyde Smith, asking the correct time. "He had the most fascinating voice over the phone," she has recalled. "And I'd always try to answer him just as impressively."

In the spring of her senior year in high school, she received another call from Mr. Smith. This time he didn't ask her for the correct time; he wanted to interview her for a job. When she appeared at the town office, where she found not only Clyde Smith but Skowhegan's other two selectmen as well, she was offered twelve dollars a week to record tax payments on the town's books. Of course, she was flattered. For a moment she hesitated, realizing that graduation was still two months away, but she accepted the job. Something could be worked out, she reasoned, to make both graduation and the job possible. It was, and Margaret finished school by studying with her teachers at night.

But she had set her sights even higher than this. She was certain that what she really wanted was to be a teacher. In September, still only eighteen years old, Margaret accepted a job at the Pitt school, about five miles from Skowhegan. It was a one-room schoolhouse, of white clapboard, and the dozen or so pupils were children of farmers living in the remote countryside. She was paid $8.50 a week, but there was little left over for her. Five dollars went to the farm family with which she boarded, and another $1.50 went to her parents, with whom she spent her weekends.

It was hard and often discouraging work. That winter was a bitter one, as Maine winters often are. Farmhouses became fortresses against the cold. The snow lay in drifts against them, or melted in the midday sun and ran off the sloping roofs to harden again in rows of stiletto-like icicles hanging from the eaves. The water of the Kennebec no longer ran free; it had, as the natives said, "Stiffened up somethin' fierce."

In the mornings Margaret bowed her head into the savage wind and trudged the half-mile to school from the farmhouse where she had rented a room. And after school she trudged back again, to spend her evenings "boning up" for the lessons she would give the next day to country children who ranged in age from six all the way up to fourteen. Even more discouraging than the physical hardships were the unresponsive children. Most of them were there simply to pass the time.

Ragged and dirty, they gave back little to this young girl who demanded so much.

In the spring Margaret Chase got an offer from the telephone company in Skowhegan. Would she come back and take a full-time job on their switchboard? *Would* she? She didn't have to think twice. "I'd decided by then that I didn't care to teach school," she says. She packed her bags and returned to Skowhegan as quickly as she could.

There she found the swift pace of events more to her taste. After working on the switchboard for only six weeks, she was offered her choice of two jobs, both of which had suddenly become available: she could take an office job, or become chief operator. It was a difficult choice, but she made a typical decision. Her friend, Pauline Green, would become chief operator if Margaret did not. So Margaret passed it up. Pauline Green is still Skowhegan's chief telephone operator. Margaret Chase set out on a new career which led eventually to a position of power and responsibility that few women before her have reached.

3

IT WAS May 14, 1930, and Margaret Chase was about to become Margaret Chase Smith. Winter had dragged on this year as usual, fading into gray spring, the scraps of its ice and snow lying for weeks on rutted roads and in forest hollows. But now spring had come at last to inland Maine. With only members of the bride and groom's immediate families present in the old house on North Avenue, Margaret Chase was married to Clyde Smith, the First Selectman whose voice had once charmed her over the telephone.

For those who looked on, it was a moving ceremony. The principals were not star-struck young lovers. Clyde Smith was fifty-four years old, and his bride thirty-three. They had known each other for years, casually at first, then more intimately as they drifted through a long courtship so common to small towns in those not-so-distant days. Attended by her sisters, Evelyn and Laura, and given in marriage by her father, Margaret made an attractive bride: she wore a dress of royal-blue lace, from Berthe's of Paris, with shoes to match and a crystal necklace. She carried a bouquet of talisman roses.

It was a new, but in many respects not an unfamiliar, life to which she committed herself when she exchanged the

vows of marriage with Clyde Smith. He had been a professional politician all his adult life. Born in the farm town of
Harmony, 20 miles northeast of Skowhegan, he had become
superintendent of schools in nearby Hartland at the age of
twenty. At twenty-one he had been a member of the state
legislature. At twenty-eight he had been elected sheriff of
Somerset County, and had moved to Skowhegan to take up
his duties. This was in the early years of the twentieth century, and Clyde Smith became known as "The Boy Sheriff."
Later he was Skowhegan's First Selectman for 16 years,
served in the State Senate, and was the publisher of the
Independent-Reporter, a weekly newspaper printed in Skowhegan.

Smith's first marriage, to Edna Page in 1907, had ended
in divorce in 1914. During his years as Skowhegan's First
Selectman, he had much to do with bringing the state's
Women's Reformatory to the town (he was later the chairman of that institution's board). He was a hard-fighting,
energetic, and daring politician. Years later Maine's Senator
Owen Brewster (who did not often share Clyde Smith's
advanced views) said of him:

"In 1923 Clyde Smith made one of the greatest speeches
of a half century in the Maine Senate in behalf of his proposal for old age pensions. It was a period when this topic
was scarcely thought of by the great mass of his fellow men."

Now, in 1930, he was still a vigorous, persuasive man with
bushy gray hair and a love for talking and arguing with
people; politics was his life. He was successful in his own
way, having never lost an election for any office. Though he
did not smoke or drink, he put away enormous quantities of
chocolate candies while engaging in another of his favorite
pastimes, poker. In answer to a question about her courtship
Margaret Smith replies:

"Mostly we went campaigning. Anyone who ever spent any time with him ended up going campaigning."

It was an activity in which Margaret Smith herself had become quite proficient. She not only had become a prominent woman in Skowhegan; her name was known throughout the state. After working at the telephone company for two years, she had resigned to take a job with Skowhegan's weekly newspaper, the *Independent-Reporter*. There, in the circulation and advertising departments, she had met important people, sold ads and become familiar with many of the other aspects of public relations work which she would put to use later on.

The paper's publisher at the time, Roland T. Patton, detected at once the valuable qualities of his new employee. He shifted her around from department to department to give her more experience ("He saw I was interested," she says) and even put her to work collecting news items. This, for her, was simple; she knew everything that was going on in town. "I could collect the news," she admits, "but I couldn't write it. I always had everybody going to Waterville shopping and coming back again. I couldn't vary the sentences."

Among her many jobs with the paper was that of accepting classified ads. One morning in 1927 a Skowhegan mill owner named Cummings came to the office to place an ad for a new office manager. The job paid fifty dollars a week. Margaret, making $28 after eight years at the paper, raised her eyebrows and asked, half jokingly, "How about me?"

Cummings was interested. He chatted with her for a while and, when he left, he had a new office manager.

"I hated to leave the newspaper business," Margaret said, "but I was nearly doubling my salary." (Neither the sentiment nor the fact is unique, as any ex-newspaperman will tell you.)

It was about this time that she began to see a great deal of Clyde Smith. She was, in a sense, in public life too. She had been a charter member of its local chapter before rising to the presidency of the State Federation of Business and Professional Women's Clubs. And, shortly before her marriage in 1930, she was asked by Skowhegan Republican leaders to accept the Somerset County Committeewoman's post of the Republican State Committee. Reluctant at first, she finally accepted, and remained a hard-working member of the committee for six years.

Though she might have had no inkling of it at the time, it was really her marriage to Clyde Smith that determined her career in politics. For the moment, she was content to help her husband with his own career. This was an exciting day in her life. After the ceremony in the modest Chase home, the wedding party moved to the groom's large house across town for a gay reception at which 250 guests toasted him and his bride. Afterward the Smiths were off on a brief honeymoon (during which, you can be sure, Clyde Smith did some campaigning, shaking hands with old friends and striking up new acquaintances) and then Margaret was back in Skowhegan—the mistress of a 30-room mansion.

Even in those years Margaret Smith spent considerable periods of time away from Skowhegan. There were frequent trips to nearby towns in her husband's black Maxwell automobile, campaigning and getting acquainted with potential voters. And there were frequent trips to the state capitol at Augusta, where Clyde Smith was a member of the governor's council. There, while the council was in session, Margaret Smith used to sit and knit in the corridors of the green-domed capitol while she waited for her husband.

A number of times during his political career Clyde Smith had been prominently mentioned in the state as a candidate for governor; 1936 was one of those years. Had he been the

Republican candidate, he surely would have been elected, for it was another Republican year in the state; only Maine and Vermont ran counter to the national tide by voting against Franklin D. Roosevelt's Democratic administration. But Maine's Republican leaders asked Smith to withdraw from the gubernatorial race and run for Congressman instead. He did, and won decisively.

Now Margaret Smith saw Washington for the first time. Though her husband was reluctant at first to put her on the payroll as his secretary, fearing he would be accused of nepotism, the people in Skowhegan wanted them there as a team. Margaret Smith had many friends in town, and they were aware of her considerable talents.

"I'm a real product of nepotism," she was to say jokingly, years later, "I wouldn't be in the Senate now if I hadn't been a member of my husband's staff."

She became his secretary, and constant companion on his campaign and research tours. In a sense she was more enthusiastic about his new position than he was. To Clyde Smith, Washington seemed a long way from his native Maine.

"He was never too happy here," she said. "He liked to have people around him who knew him . . . people who liked him and needed his help. He felt somehow out of touch in Washington."

But Margaret Smith was swept up in politics now. With her husband, who was interested in labor legislation, she traveled through the South, studying labor conditions there. She helped him with his speeches and his mail, and with the background of prospective legislation that made him one of the most informed members of the House of Representatives. Meanwhile, his health began to fade under the strain of his long years in political life. He suffered a heart attack in 1937, but recovered and won re-election to the House in 1938.

In April, 1940, Clyde Smith suffered another, more severe,

heart attack. Doubt plagued him; politics had been his life, but he didn't know whether his health would permit him to run for re-election. It was here that his physician in Washington, Dr. Paul F. Dickens, stepped in and contrived one of those simple solutions which alter other people's lives. He took Margaret Smith aside.

"Look, Margaret," Dr. Dickens said in his Georgia drawl, "Clyde is a very sick man, and the thing he surely doesn't need right now is worry. First of all, he's got to make his illness public so the people back in Maine know about it. And then he should tell them that if he isn't well enough to run for re-election, you will file in his place, and then he can ask the people to support *you*."

She was surprised, but anxious to ease her husband's mind. She agreed to the plan. On April 7, 1940, Smith released to the press the news of his illness, and of the plan to let his wife run in his place if he wasn't able to campaign. That night he suffered another heart attack. A few minutes later he was dead.

Suddenly Margaret Smith was on her own again, but in a vastly different world. It had been one thing for a lone woman to make her way in a small and isolated town. It would be quite another thing for her to set out alone, a widow now, in the demanding, savage and infinitely complex world of national politics. What were the odds against her?

The odds have always been heavy against any woman in politics. Women had wielded great power before, but it had almost always been inherited (Queen Elizabeth I, Cleopatra), won through treachery (Catherine the Great, Cleopatra) or through their men (Catherine de' Medici, Cleopatra). Even in America the few women who had served in elective offices usually had been appointed to those positions simply to fill the unexpired terms of their dead husbands. Not only was woman's ability to seek elective office comparatively new in America, but so was her right to vote: as strange as it now seems, in 1940 women had been voting throughout all of the United States for only twenty years.

The idea of woman's suffrage, of course, was far older. Mary Wollstonecraft, an Englishwoman whose daughter married Percy Bysshe Shelley, wrote the first great feminist document, "Vindication of the Rights of Women," in 1792. It created a frightful uproar, as one can imagine. American women got started somewhat later. It was in 1848, during a woman's rights convention at Seneca Falls, New York, that the suggestion that women should have the right to vote was first proclaimed to the public. This startling notion was advanced by Elizabeth Cady Stanton, an otherwise normal woman who was the wife of a politician and the mother of three small boys.

At this suggestion, a Quaker lady in the audience jumped to her feet and cried: "Why, Lizzie, thee will make us ridiculous!"

A lot of men thought so, too. Early leaders of the women's suffrage movement, such as Mrs. Stanton and Susan B. Anthony, were hooted at and insulted wherever they stood up to fight for their beliefs. The commonest remark about them was that they were sexless and perverted (which ignored the fact that many of these suffragettes were pleasant, normal women, happily married and with numerous children). Opponents of woman suffrage backed up their objections by quotations from Scripture, just as some people still find justification in Scripture for their attacks on "inferior races," the pursuit of fun, or anything else they dislike. Marion Sanders, in her book *The Lady and the Vote*, recalls that other anti-feminists, not wishing to go that far back, pointed to a passage from the writings of Thomas Jefferson:

Were our state a pure democracy there would still be excluded from our deliberations: 1) Infants, until arrived at years of discretion; 2) Women, who, to prevent depravation of morals and ambiguity of issues, could not mix promiscuously in the gatherings of men; 3) Slaves....

In the beginning the American woman suffrage movement identified itself with other causes. Women themselves had no political reality (the chief reality of American life) and so they fought for the abolition of slavery. They also got mixed up (unwisely, many thought) in the prohibition movement. Perhaps their leaders felt the need of tangible issues to go along with the abstractions of "suffrage." It was easy for them to identify with "slaves," just as it was easy for them to want to abolish the cause of drunkenness, from which they suffered, in the form of brutal husbands, so much physical and spiritual humiliation.

Yet Susan B. Anthony, an ardent teetotaler, argued that this was bad strategy for the woman suffrage movement.

"Is it not perfectly idiotic," she asked, "for us to be telling them that the first thing we shall do with our ballots will be to knock them out of their pet pleasures and vices?"

A visionary, perhaps, but a realist too.

There were many discouragements. After having worked so hard for the emancipation of the slaves, woman suffrage leaders saw male Negroes get the vote (technically, at least) after the Civil War, while they were once more ignored. Here and there a courageous state legislature passed laws giving women the right to vote in state elections. Wyoming enacted the first such law in 1869, creating so much of an uproar elsewhere that there was talk in Congress of barring that state from the Union. Wyoming prepared an official answer:

"We may stay out of the Union a hundred years, but we will come in with our women."

In 1872 a woman named Victoria Woodhull announced that she was a candidate for the Presidency on the People's party ticket. Many women wished her well, but her own mother was not among them. That sweet old party blabbed that Victoria was putting into practice her thoughts about free love by sharing her home with both her husband and her lover. The matter was thoroughly looked into. The police uncovered some free-love material which they charged she had sent through the mail and, as a result, Victoria spent election night in jail. She finished considerably behind Ulysses S. Grant and Horace Greeley in the balloting.

After the twentieth century began, women became even more aggressive. Torchlight parades and mass meetings drummed up interest in their cause. Equality in jobs, suffrage and all other matters was demanded "*now*," though of course there were "moderates" who thought that such innovations must come about slowly. One of the extremists, Lida Stokes Adams, grumbled because, in 1913, as the steamship *Titanic* was sinking, the traditional lifeboat call of "women and children first" was sounded.

"The lifeboats of the *Titanic*," she claimed, "should have been filled with an equal number of men."

Victory came at last after World War One. Women had done excellent work in offices, factories and on the farms. Men began to believe the ladies weren't such inferior creatures after all. In 1919 Congress passed the Nineteenth Amendment, giving women the right to vote. Early in 1920 the amendment had been ratified by enough states to permit women to vote that year for the first time in a Presidential election (although North Dakota made the ladies use separate ballot boxes).

By 1940 there had been a number of women in Congress, but mostly by appointment; it was believed that campaigning was too arduous and politically too dirty for women. When a Senator dies, the governor of his state appoints a successor to his post; but when a Congressman dies, a new election is held even though the regular election is only a few months away. Once Margaret Smith had committed herself as a candidate for her husband's seat, she was in for a difficult year. She waged four campaigns within seven months: there was a special primary for candidates for Clyde Smith's seat, a runoff, an election in May to fill his unexpired term, and finally the regular election in the fall to determine the Congressman from Maine's Second Congressional District for the next two years. Margaret Smith, campaigning as if her life depended on it, swept all four elections.

"I'd been taught by my husband to do it right," she said. "None of the elections was even close."

And so Margaret Smith, after disposing of the mansion in which she and her husband had spent so little time in recent years (the house was bought by a private group and converted into a hospital), tidied up her affairs in Skowhegan and once more took up her residence in Washington. It was the beginning of one of the most remarkable careers in the history of American politics.

~ 4 ~

WHEN Margaret Chase Smith entered Congress in the summer of 1940 the world was a very frightening place. World War Two had broken out in Europe the previous September. After a winter of eerie unreality, the German *Blitzkrieg,* or "lightning war," had smashed Europe's uneasy quiet. Norway, Denmark, Belgium, Luxembourg and Holland had fallen before the Nazi armies. France, too, had crumbled; Adolf Hitler had danced his insane little jig in Paris, that lost and lovely city. Now Winston Churchill's England awaited the onslaught of the Luftwaffe's massed bombers.

Americans watched from 3,000 miles away, uncertain, and quarreling among themselves like people unnerved by the approach of a violent storm. There were those who would have had us ignore the Nazis. Whatever unpleasantness existed over there (the stink of bodies burning in the ovens of German concentration camps, the cries of children trapped in London's smoking rubble) was none of our affair; let us bury our heads in the sand, they said, and maybe Hitler will go away. Others smelled the stink, and heard the cries, and thought the world too small to let America rest untouched. Among them was Margaret Chase Smith. In one of her first official duties as a Congresswoman she voted for the 1940

Selective Training and Service Act, a bill which provided for the draft of men twenty-one to thirty-five years old, who would serve for one year and bring our army up to a reasonable strength of 900,000 troops.

It was a difficult time for all Congressmen, and the burden was unusually heavy for a woman taking up the duties of her first elective office. But Margaret Smith was a resourceful woman. "I had been close to my husband while he was in Congress," she said later. "I knew everything he did, and through him I had been close to many of the Congressmen I had to work with now. So I just kept right on doing what I'd *been* doing. The only thing different was the voting."

Since there were then only seven women among the 435 members of the House, each of them had to struggle not only to be heard but to be heard respectfully. Fortunately, one of the most respected members of the House in 1940 was Mary T. Norton, a New Jersey Democrat who already had served there for sixteen years (and was to serve for ten more). A battling liberal, Mary Norton had been a leading supporter of the Wage and Hour Bill, which gave non-union workers protection against low pay and long hours. During her years in the House, she had been chairman of three different committees. A formidable woman, surely, but one who had had to earn her colleagues' respect, as every other Congresswoman did.

She had won her battle convincingly. Once, when a male representative condescendingly referred to her as "the lady," she stiffened in her chair.

"I am not *the lady*," she shot back. "I am a member of Congress, elected by the Thirteenth New Jersey District."

But Mary Norton was a woman too. She liked outrageous hats (she always regretted the House rule which prohibited its members from wearing hats on the floor) and she persisted in wearing an orchid pinned to her dress. It must have been a comfort to the other women entering Congress to find Mary Norton, who already had fought and won so many battles, there before them.

"Every move we women make is commented on," Margaret Smith said at the time. "No one cares how a man walks across the floor, but every step *we* take is noticed."

The fresh rose, held glistening in a tiny vial of water which she fastened to her dress every morning, was soon to become one of the lively discussion pieces of the House of Representatives. Once, just before she ran for her House seat, a friend had given her a rose in one of those glass vials. Delighted, she had made the rose a fixture of her daily attire.

"Sometimes in a photograph," she has said, "the rose seems more important than I do."

Now, however, this quiet, graying lady from Maine was making her mark in another way. The conflict in Europe, where gallant England held the Nazis at bay, created critical problems on this side of the Atlantic. Following one on another like waves from a tormented sea, they hurled themselves at Congress. It was then that the stubborn independence which has distinguished Margaret Smith's political career made its first appearance.

One of the most important problems confronting Congress at that time was the subject of "Lend Lease." A bill was proposed which would give President Roosevelt the power to lend or lease war supplies to nations he considered vital to the defense of the United States. To pass such an act would, of course, bring the United States closer to conflict with Germany, for England would be the chief object of this aid. The entire Maine delegation in the House, with the exception of Margaret Smith, voted against the bill; she voted for it. The Lend Lease Act was passed by Congress early in 1941.

"I got some black looks," she admitted later.

She was to get a lot more. When a bill came up which proposed to arm American merchant ships in order to be able to defend themselves against attack by planes and submarines, she broke with her party on the issue. Most Republicans voted against the bill; she voted for it. She eventually had the satisfaction of finding that these measures, particularly the Lend Lease Act, had played a vital role in the final Allied victory.

On December 7, 1941, the Japanese attacked Pearl Harbor, throwing America into the war. All Congressmen, whatever their earlier feelings, were now committed to total victory. With the great issue resolved in violence, they could attend to the more specific, yet pressing, problems which are a day-to-day part of our government.

Congress is divided into committees, in which the real work of legislation is done. Any Congressman or Senator can propose a bill, and it is then referred to the committee which deals with the affairs under which that bill comes. For example, a bill dealing with some aspect of the army would be referred to the Armed Services Committee. There the bill is hammered out in detail by the members of both parties, then sent to the floor to be voted on by the entire House. This system, though it has often been attacked as too restricting for a progressive government, has proved to be the most feasible method of getting things done in the large, and sometimes unwieldly, Congress.

Each Congressman is appointed to one or more committees, the more experienced members, of course, getting seats on the more important committees. One of the reasons for the feasibility of the committee system is that, by working intensively on committees which deal with specific areas of legislation, the Congressman can specialize and eventually become something of an expert in a few aspects of government. No one person could be expected to master all of the government's complexities; so many bills come before Congress each session that a Congressman can be expected to understand thoroughly only a few of them. Those who study the subjects with which their committees deal can make a valuable contribution to our government.

At first Margaret Smith wanted an appointment to the House Labor Committee. House Republican leaders, however, who assign members of their party to their committee places, turned down her request. Her husband had been on the Labor Committee and, though a Republican, had often voted against his party and with Chairman Mary Norton for liberal legislation. Since Margaret Smith seemed to be of her husband's persuasion, she was shunted temporarily onto the Education and Invalid Committee, which Republican leaders thought suitable for a woman (especially one of an independent nature).

But she knew the value of committee work—the right committee—for the people at home. The most successful Congressmen are those who work always with the people of their own district in mind. Representative Richard Bolling of Missouri has expressed it best:

"Congressmen work their way onto those committees where they can get favors for their districts and after that they can't be beaten in elections. They establish themselves in little enclaves of subcommittees where they are more powerful than the President."

Writer Murray Kempton tells the story of John Lindsay, the controversial young Republican from New York City who parodied this compulsion of Congressmen to vote only for their constituents' desires, and therefore often *against* the national interest. Someone noted that Lindsay had voted against certain censorship bills, which were designed to ban pornographic literature (but which some critics of the bills believed might affect "unpopular" literature as well).

"Pornography is the largest industry in my district," Lindsay said in mock seriousness. "Do they want to make it a depressed area?"

Maine, of course, has always been a seafaring state, and much of its industry is linked in one way or another with the sea. While heavy shipping there has declined, one sees in the coastal towns unmistakable signs that their people still take their living from the sea—the men in the streets, their high rubber boots turned down at the tops ... dozens of lobster traps, piled one on another in neighborhood yards ... strips of codfish strung like wet wash to dry on a line ... oilskins, clam rakes and fresh crab meat for sale in the village stores ... young Coast Guardsmen in town after a tour of duty at an offshore lighthouse—here are the descendants of those people who lived in the Maine celebrated by John Greenleaf Whittier:

> From gray sea-fog, from icy drift,
> From peril and from pain,
> The home-bound fisher greets thy lights,
> O hundred-harbored Maine.

Once, long ago, much of the timber cut from its thick forests went into the hulls of ships; its tall, sturdy white pines were coveted as masts on both sides of the Atlantic. Though shipbuilding as an industry has declined along most of the coast, there are towns where it is still important. Kittery is one, and its tradition is long and rich: John Paul Jones' ship *Ranger* was built there in 1777, and later the *Kearsage*, which won glory by sinking the dreaded Confederate cruiser *Alabama* during the Civil War.

Today the Portsmouth Naval Base, a big submarine-building and repair yard, lies on the islands at the mouth of the Piscataqua River between Kittery and Portsmouth, New Hampshire. The shipyard there is important to the economy of southern Maine. With this in mind, Margaret Smith asked for, and received, a place on the House Naval Affairs Committee in 1943. (In 1947 this committee and the House Military Affairs Committee were merged, and renamed the Armed Services Committee.) She used her position on that committee to see that Maine got its share of federal industrial contracts; this is a battle she has never stopped fighting.

"Margaret has been extremely valuable to Maine," May Craig, the political columnist, has said.

But Margaret Smith has not used her committee posts simply to fatten the pocketbooks of the people of Maine. From the very beginning she fought, too, for the right of American women, a majority group which our government often treats as an insignificant minority. She is known as the "Mother of the Waves" because of her long struggle for women's right within the armed services.

The Waves (Women Appointed for Volunteer Emergency Service) were organized in 1942 to relieve able-bodied men of their desk jobs so that they might serve where sailors really belong—at sea. One of Margaret Smith's first struggles was to have Waves approved for non-combat duties overseas. It was not a completely original idea. The Wacs (Women's Army Corps) already served overseas. And the late Admiral Robert R. Coontz recalled in his memoirs that the Yeomanettes, a World War One version of the Wacs, had applied for overseas duty:

"I had an excellent set of Yeomanettes who came from places all the way from Wyoming to Alaska," Admiral Coontz wrote. "The Alaskan girls were strong and robust, and any one of them could have licked me in an open fight. They were anxious to go to France, and the only way open to them to attain their objective was by preparing themselves to be fighters, the same as men. We organized among them several companies of infantry.

"Had the war lasted a few months longer, I feel positive they would have been accepted for service, and would have gone to France. The sight of these girls from the Northwest and Alaska going into battle would have inspired their brethren in arms."

Margaret Smith had no such Amazons in mind when, at the request of the Navy Department in 1944, she introduced a bill which would permit Waves to serve in hospitals and offices overseas. Many men in Congress seemed horrified at the idea. "They will find hardships overseas that no American woman should have to endure," one of them said.

"In that case," Margaret Smith replied, "we'd better bring all the nurses home."

The House passed the bill and, when the Senate followed, women were released for duty in Alaska, Hawaii and the Caribbean.

That same year Margaret Smith fought the Tabor Amendment, which would have cut in half the federal funds destined for community services. "I have seen children locked in cars all day because parents had no place to leave them while they worked in war plants," she said. "Services must be provided for these children."

She and six other women in the House turned the tide, and the amendment was beaten by five votes.

In addition to the satisfaction she received from working on so many worthy projects, Margaret Smith was also caught up in the excitement of the war effort. She was selected to christen a ten-thousand-ton Liberty Ship, named for another prominent New England lady, Emily Dickinson. On a voyage from Bath to Boston, she became the first woman ever to ride on an American destroyer in wartime. And in December, 1944, she took the first of the many extensive overseas trips which have kept her informed of the state of our armed forces and that of pivotal nations around the world.

The purpose of this trip, which she made in the company of ten other members of the House, was to form an overall picture of the Pacific war in preparation for legislation soon to come before Congress. The war became for her an immediate experience. She spent a day aboard a large aircraft carrier during battle practice at sea; Fleet Admiral Chester W. Nimitz was her host. Traveling 17,000 miles in eighteen days, she visited hospitals, enlisted men's quarters and naval establishments.

While she learned much about the operation of our armed forces, she also retained the personal touch. Returning, she had a tip for those mothers who kept their fighting sons abreast of local happenings: soldiers and sailors overseas, she said, often had to wait months to receive the newspapers and magazines shipped to them from America. If, however, their mothers and wives clipped pertinent items and mailed them in the same envelopes with their letters, the boys would get them much faster. Many a long, pompous report of an official overseas inspection tour has contained information less useful than this was.

Back in Congress Margaret Smith continued to astonish, and sometimes amaze, her colleagues with her voting independence. Conditioned partly by her husband's views, and partly by her own memories of the low salaries paid to workers in her home state, she was far more liberal than most of her fellow Republicans who acted on labor and welfare legislation. She voted with the Democrats against the Smith-Connally Anti-Strike Act, against a bill to freeze the social security tax, and *for* federal pay raises.

Peace came in 1945. There was new hope now for mankind, hopes which Russia's intransigence and aggressiveness later dimmed. The U. S., having got rid of one madman in Hitler, now was confronted with another in its former ally, Joseph Stalin. Yet the United Nations promised much for the

future. It was formed near the end of the war to succeed
the old League of Nations, which had failed to keep a permanent peace after World War One. This seemed to be
civilization's last chance.

Margaret Smith spoke out in favor of the infant organization right from the beginning. "It is a symbol of the greatest
advance in the march of civilization," she said. "It is the hope
that we can keep the peace. It is the hope that our human
progress will catch up with our machine progress."

She voted also for the European Recovery Plan, having
become convinced that the path to real safety in the modern
world was not in the narrow isolationism then typical of so
many members of her party. But, in 1947, when she voted
against a Republican-sponsored cut in President Truman's
budget, she ruffled some important feathers. A story went out
over the wires that the only Republican voting against the
cut was "Representative Smith of Maine." The conservative
Chicago *Tribune* countered with a blistering editorial about
administrative extravagance. It closed, nearly spluttering,
with the warning: "Whoever that Congressman from Maine
was he should be read out of the party."

There were charges that Margaret Smith was a Democrat
masquerading as a Republican, and hints that she was simply
being perverse. She firmly rejected both descriptions.

"I don't really vote against my party that often," she said.
"But I've gotten the reputation of being a liberal because I
cast those votes on some very dramatic issues."

When she voted with the Republicans and the conservative Democrats for the Taft-Hartley Act (which clamped
down on Labor) in 1947, her critics within the party were
somewhat mollified. But they continued to look on her with
some suspicion, as one might in circling a skittish mare.

Margaret Smith's battle to win equal rights for American
women in the peacetime armed forces went doggedly on.

After hearing complaints by army nurses that they received poor treatment compared with that given male officers in overseas positions, she pressed a vigorous investigation to set matters right. She also pushed through legislation granting nurses permanent rank, rather than simply reserve status, in the armed forces.

Representative Carl Vinson of Georgia, the chairman of the House Armed Services Committee, was the gentleman who was kept under almost constant pressure by the persistent Margaret Smith.

"When a woman gets a bill in her bonnet," Vinson said, "she worries over it just like it was a baby."

Congressmen's junkets have fallen into disrepute in recent years chiefly because certain members have abused the privilege, squandering the taxpayers' money by touring in the manner of Oriental potentates. These overseas trips, however, have had some advantages for the taxpayer too. Responsible and alert members of Congress have detected (and so have been able to correct) many flagrant instances of the waste of American funds abroad. Others have added to their knowledge of world conditions and thus have become better equipped to vote wisely when legislation pertaining to those areas comes up in Congress.

Margaret Smith made her first extensive peacetime trip abroad in 1947, visiting 16 countries in Asia, Africa and Europe. In Iran she became the first woman to address the national legislature. The most exciting (or hair-raising) moment came on the final leg of her journey. The plane carrying the Congressional party developed engine trouble over the Atlantic Ocean, 700 miles west of the Azores. The pilot turned the plane around, headed for the Azores with one engine dead, and passed the word for the passengers to put on their Mae West life preservers in case he was forced to ditch at sea.

The passengers were more than a little nervous. Margaret Smith, however, broke open a box of harmonicas she had bought as souvenirs in Switzerland and passed them around to her colleagues. Then she joined them in singing old songs, spiced with wisecracks, and the tension was gone.

"She was the calmest person on the plane," one of her admiring colleagues said after they had landed safely in the Azores.

A more pleasant thrill was in store for her upon her return to Washington. She was the principal subject of a letter sent to the State Department from the United States Embassy in Iran. It read in part:

> The impression created by Mrs. Margaret Chase Smith should be especially mentioned. Government officials here as well as Iranian deputies were particularly enthusiastic regarding Mrs. Smith, not only because of her personal intelligence and charm, but also as a representative of American womanhood.

A year later, when Margaret Smith was running for the Senate, Representative Gordon Canfield of New Jersey was to stand up on the floor of the House and recall that trip in a flowery tribute.

"We doff our hats to her for the contributions she made toward the success of our mission everywhere," Canfield said. "The barefooted, ill-dressed, undernourished German tots in the Russian sector of Berlin loved this woman from America who pressed lollypops into their hands. Our troops cheered her at our military installations. . . . You should have seen her climbing the stony hillsides back of Trieste as she visited our boys at the roadblocks on the Yugoslav border."

There were now in the House women who could be called more "glamorous" than Margaret Smith. There was, for instance, Clare Boothe Luce, actress, playwright and wife of

Henry Luce, the founder of the vast Time-Life magazine empire. And there, too, was Helen Gahagan Douglas, the charming wife of movie actor Melvyn Douglas. Yet Margaret Smith had an appeal to the public which was grounded on something deeper than "glamour." She had learned much in the House of Representatives, had conducted herself with dignity, and had been an effective pleader for the people back home in Maine. They responded by re-electing her to Congress three times—in 1942, 1944, and 1946.

Though quiet, and scrupulously avoiding the gimmicks with which many politicians get their names in the papers, she knew the value of publicity. Speaking before a group of leading Republican women at Washington in 1947, she urged them to attract more women to the party through the use of "daytime radio serials based on everyday life."

Women consistently listen to radio soap operas, she told them, adding that they could expect little interest to be stimulated by "sterile and stilted speeches at night when women have less time to listen because their families are at home." An exciting drama, in which the good life is shown to have been achieved through political activity, would be far more effective.

The suggestion provoked comment, favorable and otherwise, all over the country. Yet the frequency with which her name was being heard was not a result of the novel campaign plan. Rather, the story demanded attention because it had been presented by a woman whose name was beginning to matter. Bigger things obviously were in store for her.

ᕽᕽ 5 ᕽᕽ

THE decision had been made, and the campaign lay ahead of her. She stood alone, apparently a vulnerable target. Even now her opponents, not yet ready to speak in their own behalf, moved to smother her candidacy under doubt and ridicule.

"The little lady has simply stepped out of her class," a Maine politician (who asked not to be identified) told a reporter. "The Senate is big-league stuff. Nobody in Maine can get into the Senate without a political machine, fat campaign funds, the right business connections and the help of the powers-that-be. Margaret hasn't got any of these things."

It was the summer of 1947. The Margaret whose chances this faceless politician had so windily and cheerily discounted was Margaret Smith of Skowhegan. She had just lobbed a particularly shocking though figurative firecracker into the well-ordered political world which Maine's Republican leaders had very industriously put together.

It had all begun simply enough. A short time before, Wallace H. White, the senior United States Senator from Maine and the majority leader of the Senate, revealed that he would not seek re-election in 1948. The state's leading politicians rolled up their sleeves for action; all of them coveted the elderly Republican's seat, and a lively but routine political battle was forecast.

Then Margaret Smith entered the picture. Popular with the voters in Maine's Second Congressional District and secure in her position after seven years in the House, she was confronted by a decision which would alter the course of her life. She had done her work well in the House and now felt she merited a chance for a place in the Senate. But if the chance were to be hers, she would have to take it alone. Though a lifelong Republican, she was thought to be too "progressive" by the fossilized leaders of her party in Maine; they could think of a number of other candidates they would rather watch succeed to Senator White's vacant seat.

One of Margaret Smith's qualities is directness, which distinguishes her from most of her colleagues in the business of politics. When weighing the statement of a politician, one generally can interpret it only by reading between the lines. Margaret Smith invariably expresses *real thoughts*—incorrect thoughts, sometimes, according to her critics, but genuinely believed, and unadorned. Having decided that she was qualified for the Senate, and therefore a candidate, she made her decision public on June 1, 1947.

Even her friends were shaken. Maine's Republican primaries were more than a year away. To announce one's candidacy so far in advance was to fly in the face of traditional political practice. Her friends warned her that all the other candidates for the prized Senate seat would have that much longer now to combine forces and tear her down. But burning her bridges held no terrors for Margaret Smith; it never does for the person who doesn't look back.

"It's only fair to announce my intentions now," she said. "That way, the people who may be thinking about running for my old seat in the House will have a chance to make up *their* minds."

The odds against her were terrific. She was breaking new ground in the long struggle for women's rights. Six women had preceded her in the Senate but none had entered it by the frontal assault now planned by Maine's Congresswoman. Five had been appointed by their state governors to fill the unexpired terms of Senators who had died in office, and another had won an "interim" election and served two months there until the next regular election came around. For the most part these women were obscure in politics, and had received the appointment only because party leaders believed they would step aside quietly when asked to and let the men take over.

One of them, Mrs. Rose McConnell Long of Louisiana, was appointed to fill the unexpired term of her husband, Huey Long, who had been assassinated. She served less than a year. Her son Russell eventually won election to the Senate, so that a father, mother and son had all held the same seat. Another woman, Mrs. Hattie Caraway of Arkansas, was appointed to her late husband's seat in 1931. Then with backing of the state Democratic machine, she was elected for two more terms. She left little record behind her after 14 years in the Senate, but she was a pleasant little lady and everybody spoke well of her.

The one woman who might have made a permanent mark in the Senate was Eleanor Roosevelt. She was offered the Democratic nomination for a Senate seat from New York in 1946, a year after the death of her husband, Franklin D. Roosevelt, but she turned it down. She was an astute politician, having become interested in politics after her husband was stricken with infantile paralysis in 1921. FDR's friend Louis Howe suggested that she keep alive her husband's interest in politics. Otherwise, Howe told her, FDR might become a hopeless invalid. She interested herself in his affairs and, when he was able to get back into politics, assisted him in many ways, especially after he became President. But she was not interested in running for elective office. She had little confidence in herself.

"I have no talents, no experience, no training for anything," she once said. "If I had to go out and earn my own living I doubt I'd even make a good cleaning woman."

Margaret Smith had made a more realistic appraisal of her own talents. In Maine, the battle lines had been drawn. Until now Republican leaders there had believed that by dangling the state's governorship before her like a bright toy they might distract her from running for the Senate. Their reasoning was simple: in the governor's mansion at Augusta her wayward independence would be checked by the conservative state legislature. But Margaret Smith would not be distracted. She wanted to be a senator, not a governor.

It was a far more challenging task for her than simply battling what was at the time a weak Democratic party. She would have to fight her own party first. And since she could campaign for only one office at a time, she must withdraw from the race for her seat in the House. A defeat would probably put an end to her political career.

One of her most outspoken enemies within the Republican party was Maine's other Senator, Owen Brewster. That deep-dyed conservative believed that in Margaret Smith's case, a woman's place was in the House.

"She has been a New Dealer right from the start," Brewster said, summoning up the most frightful specter in his imaginative store.

There were two strong factions within Maine's Republican party, neither of which wanted to see Margaret Smith leave the House for the Senate. One faction favored Horace A. Hildreth, who was just completing his second two-year term as governor. The other favored Sumner Sewall, who had served two terms as governor immediately preceding Hildreth, and who had never lost an election. Both men were wealthy, college-educated, and skilled vote-getters. Both men announced their candidacy for Senator White's vacant seat and entered the Republican primary (scheduled for June, 1948) to determine the party's representative in the final election against the Democrats two months later.

Margaret Smith's third opponent in the Republican primary was the Reverend Albion Beverage, a Congregationalist minister quite as imposing as his name. His spellbinding oratory and deep-seated suspicion of any idea that smacked of internationalism had made him the darling of a certain segment of Maine's female population. The Reverend Beverage drew a provincial bead on Margaret Smith.

Having announced her candidacy early, she was still unable to take advantage of the head start in beginning her campaign. She lost valuable time when, during that interval between Congressional sessions which legislators traditionally devote to their next election campaigns, she made her tour through Europe and the Middle East with other members of the House of Representatives. She felt that because international affairs played an increasingly larger part in the day-to-day business of running the government she owed it to her constituents to study conditions around the globe in as close detail as possible. Upon returning to the United States she was more convinced than ever that her vote in the House for the European Recovery Program (how the isolationists back in Maine hated her for that!) had been correct.

By this time the 1948 session of Congress was underway. Already behind schedule on her campaign, Margaret Smith entered the Senate race without either a party machine or an organized campaign fund behind her. Her brightest asset was her record in Congress; she felt she could take that to the people with pride and confidence. And it was the people who would decide the issue.

Her schedule, always busy, now became arduous. Her three opponents in the Republican primary were based in Maine. She spent the week performing her duties at the Capitol in Washington, and returned to Maine for the weekends.

It was dead winter now, a Maine winter, and her weekly trip was long and tiring. She had to complete her flight from Washington in stages, because there were no direct flights from there to Maine. Arriving in Portland, she was still a hundred miles from her home in Skowhegan. Frequent blizzards clogged the roads. Yet, at the end of the journey, in the old white frame house on North Avenue where she had been born, her mother waited with a pot of baked beans or a steaming fish chowder. Then, in the morning, she would set out on her rounds, driving her car through the snow-walled corridors that were the neighboring roads and, later, through the slush of Maine's gray spring.

There was a lot of catching up to do. The old guard politicians, who hated her for spurning their offer of the governorship and who wanted now to see her career ruined, began to spread the kind of stories a lone and fiercely independent woman is prey to. One of the most frequently heard stories was that she "followed the Communist line." This, as her friends knew, was nonsense; the Reds couldn't control Margaret Smith, any more than the Republican party bosses could.

With characteristic persistence, the rumormongers followed this up with the charge that her votes on the various bills before Congress conflicted with Republican party thinking more than 30 percent of the time. She destroyed this contention by opening the record: she had voted with her party 95 percent of the time. Now the charges grew even more specific. She had voted against further appropriations for the House Un-American Activities Committee (that committee whose record, as one prominent political writer, Murray Kempton, once said, "has always been disgusting").

Margaret Smith phrased it a little differently, but her point was the same. "Certainly I have opposed the appropriation," she said, "because I think the time has come to put those investigations back where they belong—in the hands of the FBI."

She was opposed during her campaign by the power companies, the railroads, and most of the large corporations. Bankers and the directors of these corporations were openly against her, even writing letters which urged their friends to vote for Hildreth or Sewall in opposition to Margaret Smith. The Reverend Beverage found warm support among those women who had been outraged by Margaret Smith's votes in Congress for European aid and universal military training. ("It was my hardest decision. It had to do with so many human beings and it meant so much to so many families," she said after she had voted to extend the draft.)

Even her old boss at the woolen mill, Willard Cummings, said he would have to vote against her in the primary because she favored reciprocal trade agreements (which mill owners thought would hurt their business). "But I hate to do it," he added quickly.

Suddenly she found that she had many friends too. One of the most heartwarming gestures of support were the letters written to Maine voters by members of the business and professional women's clubs in Iran, whom she had so impressed on her overseas trip the year before. Closer to home, the wives of the very bankers and corporation directors who opposed her came forth with their support; many served in her campaign voluntarily, even paying their own expenses. Telephone operators, remembering she had once been one of them, gave her that extra bit of service when she placed long-distance calls.

There was a letter from an eighteen-year-old girl, enclosing a dollar bill: "I regret only two things—that this must be merely a token contribution to your Senatorial campaign, and that I am not yet old enough to vote."

She had never solicited money for her Congressional campaigns, preferring to pay the expenses out of her own pocket, but now friends prevailed on her to let them begin limited fund drives. Even so, few large checks were gathered; her campaign fund was built chiefly of small contributions, ten dollars or less. This proved to be more of an advantage than a disadvantage; she openly derided the wealth of, and behind, her opponents. It cast her in the role of underdog, fighting the rich and the powerful.

The rumors and innuendoes persisted. A woman working for one of the other candidates charged that Margaret Smith had constantly followed the "CIO line" in Congress. Not afraid to be linked with labor, Margaret Smith immediately turned this attack to her own advantage. She had believed for a long time that the Republicans must take the play away from the Democrats in this field and plan a long-range labor program.

"You cannot legislate labor out of the picture, as a lot of people would like to do," she said. "The public doesn't always understand all the problems involved in labor, and it is Congress's responsibility to lead it."

Some of the charges against her, though potentially harmful, were downright silly. One of her opponents dug up a picture that had been taken during her 1947 trip to Europe. It was a Signal Corps photo, in which she was shown visiting American sailors stationed in Trieste. On the table in front of the sailors were several cans of beer.

"Look at her," her opponents said, passing around the picture. "There she is . . . boozing it up with a gang of sailors!"

This could have hurt her in Maine, long a Prohibition stronghold (and the first state in the Union to adopt a comprehensive Prohibition law in the nineteenth century). Fortunately, Margaret Smith's friends knew she never smoked or drank. Again, she turned this inept attack against her opponents, charging she was being "smeared." But mostly she campaigned on her own record in Congress. "The Can-Do Candidate with the Can-Did Record," her campaign literature described her, and followed up with the slogan: "Don't Trade a Record for a Promise."

Even during the brief periods she was able to remain in Skowhegan that spring she was constantly busy. There were long-distance phone calls to Washington, during which she dictated letters and gave instructions to her staff. There were visits from local people who wanted to ask a favor of her: could she help a widow get her pension straightened out? Or help a youngster get an appointment to the Naval Academy at Annapolis? She made notes of the requests, and did her best to fulfill them.

Another example of her ability to turn disaster into good fortune took place on Friday, February 13. Stepping out of a car while rushing to keep an appointment, she slipped on the ice and broke her right arm. Friends rushed her to Eastern Maine General Hospital, where the fractured arm was set and placed in a cast. After a brief rest, she continued that same afternoon to Rockland, 60 miles away, where she made a speech before a men's service club. That evening she made another speech in a Portland suburb, 90 miles from Rockland.

The immediate obstacle thrown up by the injury was that she could no longer drive her own car. But volunteers quickly came forward, and through the remainder of the campaign (during most of which her arm was in a cast) she was driven wherever she wanted to go. One of her drivers, a husky man who took her through the vast potato-growing lands of Aroostook County, said of her:

"I never saw anybody with so much energy. I was all worn out while she was still going strong."

Her schedule was rather frantic, because she had so little time in which to campaign. Big towns and small—Readfield . . . Winthrop . . . East Livermore . . . Dixfield . . . Lewiston . . . Rumford . . . Auburn—were on her list, and she made them all.

She was her own campaign manager. Most of her appearances were arranged by a hasty telephone call. Then she would get in her car, sharing space with cardboard placards and a red hatbox in which she carried Vote for Margaret Smith buttons and her campaign literature, and off she would go. There were few big rallies for her. She spoke chiefly to smaller groups, gathered to hear her in a town library, a firehouse or a school. She spoke, too, before schoolchildren. Though her audiences then were unable to vote, she knew they might influence their parents, and someday they themselves would vote. At such times she avoided any reference to her candidacy.

"I'd tell the children about my duties in Congress, and about Congress itself," she said. And, when she spoke of good citizenship, she skillfully worked in, as illustrations, the measures she had pushed during her years in Congress.

A campaign is a wearing physical experience which affects candidates for public office in many ways. California's Pat Brown has said that he shakes hands so often during a campaign that he must take shots to relieve the pain in the sensitive muscles near his right elbow. Margaret Smith, her right arm already in a cast, was spared this ordeal, but she was constantly "on stage" and she had to be polite to *everybody*.

Many of the people she met were friendly. At other times she would walk up to a man on the street, smile and say: "I'm Margaret Smith from Skowhegan. Do you know me?"

And receive the blunt reply: "Nope. Can't say that I do."

"Well, I'm your representative in Congress," she would say, "and now I'm running for United States Senator."

Some encounters were mildly aggravating. Approaching a couple of burly men at work in a lumberyard one day, she introduced herself pleasantly. There was no answer. She continued to talk to them for a few minutes but, since they showed no evidence that they were paying any attention to her, she turned around and, still smiling, walked away.

But there were amusing incidents in compensation. After she had talked about Congress to some schoolchildren in Jackman, the father of one of the boys came to her with a question.

"What's all this you've been giving my six-year-old son?" he asked. "He says you told the kids about a great big house in Washington where all the men sit on the floor. Now he won't sit on a chair at home—he wants to sit on the floor all the time."

The primary was in doubt until the final weekend, when Margaret Smith went home to Skowhegan to catch up on some Congressional paperwork and await the results. The primary itself took place on Monday, June 21.

"We thought we had a chance until that final weekend," a prominent supporter of Horace Hildreth said. "Then people all over the state seemed to sense that Margaret Smith was going to win. They jumped on her bandwagon, and our campaign came apart at the seams."

Women came out to vote in unprecedented numbers. The city clerk of Portland reported that more women had voted than ever before in the city's history. On the little island of Matinicus, in the Atlantic Ocean twenty miles off Rockland, sixty-one people voted; Margaret Smith got all the votes. All over the state the results told a similar story. It was Margaret Smith by a landslide.

The overwhelming quality of her victory against powerful opposition stunned Maine's political experts. The final totals were 63,786 for Margaret Smith, 30,949 for Hildreth, 21,763 for Sewall and only 6,399 for the unfortunate Reverend Beverage. Margaret Smith had polled more votes than her three opponents put together.

Telegrams and phone calls poured into the old house in Skowhegan. With her smiling mother at her side, she accepted the congratulations of her friends and neighbors.

"I couldn't have done it without the help of people like you," she told them.

Her eyes were tired, but she smiled often, the dimple prominent on her cheeks.

"If Margaret Smith wanted to be President," one woman in town said, "I bet she could be elected."

Still, she had the election itself ahead of her. Yet now she was an overwhelming favorite to win. Her Democratic opponent in the fall was Dr. Adrian Scolten, a Portland skin specialist. Maine's election day was September 13, the earliest in the nation. On that day, Margaret Smith won by the biggest majority ever given a Maine candidate, burying Dr. Scolten with 71.3 percent of the total vote. She had become the first woman to win her seat in the United States Senate, the first woman ever to serve in both houses of Congress, and (ironically, because of the bosses' opposition) the first woman the Republican party had put in the Senate.

In the days after the election she did not share the wild confidence her victory had encouraged in Republicans throughout the country. The old slogan, "As Maine goes, so goes the nation," was brought up again by those who believed Margaret Smith's victory foreshadowed that of Thomas E. Dewey over Democrat Harry Truman in the Presidential elections to be held in November. Margaret

Smith, who had studied Maine's election returns, urged her Republican colleagues to be careful.

"Based on my figures," she said, "the Presidential election will be won by the Democrats, unless things suddenly change. We Republicans will have to roll up our sleeves and fight."

Margaret Smith proved to be one of the nation's few political prophets that fall. Harry Truman beat the overconfident Dewey in November in the biggest election upset of our time. No wonder Ohio's Senator Robert A. Taft, the Republican party's unchallenged leader in the Senate, said of the new Senator from Maine:

"Margaret Smith is the Joan of Arc of the Republican party, who may well lead us out of the morass of defeat."

Behind the hyperbole was a profound conviction that Margaret Chase Smith was neither an ordinary politician nor an ordinary woman. She would play a historic role in the greatest deliberative institution political man has yet devised.

~ 6 ~

Margaret Chase Smith was sworn in as a United States Senator on January 3, 1949. The ceremony took place before a crowded gallery in the Senate Chamber on the second floor of the Capitol's north wing. Though she represented, in population, one of the Union's smaller states (just under one million people, then as now), there is no doubt that she had drawn the great crowd to the Capitol. Women had come from all over the country to see the first of their sex join what had been called for so long "the most exclusive gentlemen's club in the world."

The Senate, which began as a compromise, remains a unique institution. At the time our government was formed the larger states of the Union wanted representation according to population so that, naturally, they would send more representatives to Congress. The smaller states wanted equal representation, no matter what their population (just as in the General Assembly of the United Nations today a vote by tiny Mali equals a vote by the United States or the Soviet Union). A compromise was worked out. The men who wrote the Constitution decided that there should be *two* houses of Congress—one, the House of Representatives, in which the number of a state's representatives would depend upon its population, and the other, the Senate, in which each state would have two representatives.

The Senate, born in mistrust of bigness and "majorities," has leaned toward exclusiveness. It lends dignity to the smaller states, just as the UN, by granting Mali, for instance, or Luxembourg, a vote equal to that of the giant powers such as the United States or the Soviet Union, has given tiny and undeveloped nations a place in the world. Here "bigness" ceases to count. States whose populations are enormous (like New York and California) can't gang up on smaller states (like Rhode Island or Nevada), because a vote of the smaller fellow carries equal weight. As we shall see later, the filibuster is another weapon used by minority states or geographical sections to keep from being overwhelmed by greater numbers. The South has always wanted to preserve the Senate's exclusiveness because each Senator's vote carries more weight in a limited body. For most of our history, in fact, a Senate seat was considered too precious to let the common people vote for it: Senators, until 1913, were elected by the state legislatures, a policy, as James Madison phrased it, "of refining the popular appointment by successive filtrations." The Seventeenth Amendment provided for the popular election of Senators.

This feeling of exclusiveness has determined the way in which the Senate functions. It does not work, as in institutions of unwieldy size, by massing great numbers and engaging in pitched battle; it functions by more subtle methods, respecting each other's views and gaining a point through negotiation rather than frontal assault.

"The art of high negotiation is an absolutely necessary part of Senatorial equipment," William S. White has written in his study of the Senate, *Citadel.* "For the Institution, as it was at the beginning, is something more than a parliamentary body engaged upon parliamentary work. It is likewise an assemblage of diplomatists, in which each state in a sense sends Ambassadors to the Federal Republic, and the function of Ambassadors is not to reach proud, violent disagreement; it is, of course, to find acceptable agreement."

The Senate can never really be repudiated. Other parts of our government—an administration, or (theoretically) the whole House of Representatives—can be turned out of office at one election. Because Senators are elected for six-year terms, and because only about one-third of them come up for election at any one time, the one-third may be singled out for public retribution; but the others' terms do not expire then for two years, or four years, and public outrage is seldom long sustained.

The Senate has rights through which it exercises tremendous power. It has the right, among others, to accept or reject treaties, to accept or reject a President's appointments to the Bench or to his Cabinet, and to try impeachments (only the House can *bring* impeachments), even against the Supreme Court or the President himself. "Has it not an Authority over all the acts of the Executive?" James Monroe asked, speaking of the Senate. "What are the acts which the President can do without them?"

Many Senators feel that not even the Presidency is a higher job—it is simply a *different* job. It is no wonder that, under such responsibility, Senators react in different ways. Woodrow Wilson (a President who came to grief at the Senate's hands) probably expressed it best when he said that some Senators grow in office, others "just swell."

The public is sometimes outraged by what it considers the Senate's arrogant, money-wasting leisure in proceeding with public business. Yet the Senate's deliberation in the face of the public's demand for swift action often averts hasty, ill-considered legislation which the whole country eventually might come to regret. And the very windiness which is often ridiculed in Senators is not entirely to be censured either. It is only the "deliberative bodies" of the totalitarian countries which rush into law (rubber-stamp is a better phrase) the proposals of its leaders; Hitler's Reichstag seldom wasted any time in debate or criticism. This is the hallmark of the great democracies. In his book, *Two Cheers for Democracy*, E. M. Forster said of England's Parliament that it is often sneered at because it is a "talking shop." Forster wrote:

> I believe in it *because* it is a talking shop. I believe in the Private Member who makes himself a nuisance. He gets snubbed and is told that he is cranky or ill-informed, but he does expose abuses which would otherwise never have been mentioned, and very often an abuse gets put right just by being mentioned.... Whether Parliament is either a representative body or an efficient one is questionable, but I value it because it criticises and talks, and because its chatter gets widely reported.

And so with the United States Senate. It seems to blunder along at times, without purpose or direction, but the individual Senators are picking up bits and threads of information and storing them for future use. Even the traditional end-of-the-session rush, when bills are pushed through at a rate that seems to preclude responsible consideration, is generally the result of long months of listening and thinking, suddenly crystallized in a spasm of activity.

The charge that Congress (Senate or House) wastes great sums of money does not bear up under close examination. Listen to James Burnham, author of *Congress and the American Tradition:*

For the legislature of the richest nation in the world, the congressional budget seems modest enough by today's standards: about a hundred million dollars annually for the whole legislative establishment—a fraction of one percent of the executive budget, and much less than the expenses of hundreds of private corporations. Members of Congress, most of whom work from twelve to sixteen hours daily, are paid the salary of junior executives in a small company [$22,500 a year—both Senators and Congressmen], less than Cabinet members or Supreme Court justices, less than a tenth that of the junior officers of a big corporation.

The Senate's members are bound together by its exclusiveness, the prestige of its individual members and its long tradition that to push political differences too far is both useless in the current case, and unwise for future cases. As William S. White has said: "To grant to one's opponent in high political discussion and maneuver each and all of the right that one demands for himself—this is, uniquely in this country certainly, and perhaps in all the world, a Senate rule."

It is, in a real sense, an exclusive gentlemen's club. Many of its members are wealthy, most of them are well-educated (about half of today's Senators are lawyers) and nearly all of them abide by, and fiercely defend, the traditions that are a part of any ancient "club." It was into this club of 95 clannish men that Margaret Smith, a fifty-one-year-old woman, neither a college graduate nor a "reliable" party member, walked in January, 1949.

There is no doubt that, though there was a display of gallantry all around her, she was not taken into the clan—and that was the way she preferred it. She did not want to be taken as a woman, or as a Republican; she just wanted to be the best Senator she possibly could. According to Webster's Unabridged Dictionary, a lady Senator is a Senatrix, and two lady Senators are Senatrices, which rhymes with slices. Margaret Smith has always said, "Call me Senator." She doesn't even like "Mrs. Smith," pointing out that you don't call a male Senator "Mister." Above all, you don't call her "Maggie." Two authors who did were, as we shall see, sued by her for one million dollars (though not specifically because they called her "Maggie").

Even so, there must have been difficult moments for her when she entered the Senate. The Democrats, of course, are never happy to see another Republican enter the "club"— and it is mostly the Southern Democrats who are the leaders, acknowledged or not, of the institution. And, of course, she had done nothing to endear herself to the "Old Guard" Republicans. One of the most powerful of that group was her own fellow Senator from Maine—the aging Owen Brewster ("I can't understand what people were thinking of," he remarked after her victory in the primaries. "She has been a New Dealer right from the start").

Brewster, however, soon tried to jump on the bandwagon. After her election to the Senate was a certainty, he made public a letter he had written, urging party leaders to place "Senator Smith" on the Republican Policy Committee. Some of the luster was taken off that letter when it was revealed that Senator Robert A. Taft of Ohio, the Republican leader in the Senate, had made up his mind to do just that some time before he received Senator's Brewster's suggestion.

In a sense, of course, Capitol Hill was nothing new to Margaret Smith. "Washingtonians are transients in mind and spirit," correspondent James Reston has written, but Margaret Smith had spent so much of her time there in the last dozen years, first with her husband and then alone, that the Potomac was as familiar to her as the Kennebec. She received her set of three rooms in the old Senate Office Building, as all freshman Senators did (those from the bigger states got an extra room, usually in the basement) and began to adjust herself to her new routine.

Because Senators are habitually suspicious of change, the presence of a woman in their midst presented problems that seemed almost insurmountable. All of the Senate's facilities for comfort and recreation had been designed for men; no women allowed. Margaret Smith, it seemed, had to make the best of an embarrassing situation. Since there was no rest room provided for lady Senators, she either had to make the trip back to the Senate Office Building (on the little underground railway which connects it with the Capitol) or queue up with visitors to the Senate in front of the public washroom on the floor below the Senate Chamber. Sometimes her colleagues saw her sitting on the steps, powdering her nose.

"I don't mind using the public washroom," she said during a discreet discussion of the matter with Senator Carl Hayden of the Committee on Rules and Administration, "but I just don't have the time to stand in line without missing a roll call. And I don't want to push in front of anybody in line."

Senator Hayden said he understood perfectly, but there was nothing he could do about it.

Frustrated on that point, she asked if there was anything that could be done about the dingy cream paint on the walls of her office. Several offices, including that of Rhode Island's venerable Senator Theodore Green, were painted a more pleasing green.

"Well," Senator Hayden said, "Senator Green is an exception, because his name is Green."

Senator Hayden was so kind and shy she hated to press the point, but— He finally compromised and had her private office painted green, while leaving the other two rooms (her staff had no objection) the original dull cream. Eventually

Senate leaders came around to conceding her the other point: she was given a key to the Capitol washroom used by their wives.

She still could not use the other facilities open to gentlemen Senators—the barbershop, for instance, and the swimming pool and gymnasium. She accepted this graciously.

"I am proud," she said, "that I cost the American taxpayers less money than any of the other Senators."

There were compensations, too. She solved the problem of entertaining, which troubles every lone woman in Washington. She simply invited her guests to eat with her in the Senate dining room. "If I have done nothing else in the Senate," she said at the time, "I have got them to make a good fruit salad there."

Though her duties as a freshman Senator brought her piles of work she had never dreamed of facing, she even found the time for outside jobs. She decided it would be nice to have a television set in her office. Senator Homer Capehart of Indiana, a manufacturer of radio and television sets, had also wanted a set in his office, but he had been dissuaded upon learning that the direct current used in the Senate Office Building made it impossible. Being a woman, Margaret Smith never considered the difficulties. With the help of her new legislative assistant, Col. William C. Lewis, she put together a TV set from a do-it-yourself kit, then found a convertor which changed direct current into alternating current. The set created quite a sensation among her colleagues.

She also ventured into journalism, beginning a newspaper column, *Washington and You,* which was distributed five days a week by the United Features Syndicate. Here, too, she demonstrated the same independence of thought which has distinguished her political career. Despite the fact that hunting is one of Maine's most popular recreations, and out-of-state hunters supply a large part of Maine's tourist income, she got something off her chest.

"My opinion may be unpopular," she wrote in her column, "but I am very tired of seeing car after car with slain deer strapped to the fenders and hoods.... I don't see how a hunter can level his gun against the sad eyes of a deer and shoot to kill. What sport is there in this?"

And, of course, there was business to attend to. Though she has never made many Congressional speeches, or issued statements just for the sake of being heard, she felt impelled to appeal to Holland's Queen Juliana on January 4, 1949, a day after she had been sworn in as Maine's junior Senator. The reason for Margaret Smith's appeal was the fighting which had broken out between the Dutch and the Indonesians. The occasion was a speech before the National Federation of Business and Professional Women's Clubs, in which she said, "The potency of the United Nations is threatened by renewed fighting in the Dutch-Indonesian war. Queen Juliana, by her individual decision, can prove to the world the will and power of women for peace. Women of the world are on trial."

Although the embattled troops did not throw down their arms at the sound of this distant foreign voice, an agreement was signed at The Hague between the Netherlands and Indonesia later that year.

Margaret Smith's first public distinction in the Senate came on February 22, 1949. On that day the reading by a prominent Senator of Washington's Farewell Address is a Senate tradition. Vice-President Alben W. Barkley (a Democrat, incidentally), acting in his dual role of President of the Senate, invited Margaret Smith to read the address on this Washington's Birthday.

Margaret Smith had a word of advice for her own party

too. She said that the Republicans had lost five straight Presidential elections because they had become, in the public's mind, the party of big business. The party which adopts moderation, she predicted, will be the party of the future. Encouraging women to take a greater part in their country's politics, she reminded them that an almost one hundred percent turnout of Italian women in the recent crucial elections in Italy had saved that country from Communism.

She created a minor sensation a little later that year when she told the press that "the party which nominates a woman for the Vice-Presidency in 1952 will win the election." Since the best-known woman then holding public office was Margaret Smith, this touched off a small boom for her. There would be further reverberations in 1952.

Her name was now nationally known. Though she spoke seldom, every word she uttered was picked up and repeated in newspapers and magazines. Throwing her support to a proposal to publicize more intensively the problem of juvenile delinquency, she remarked: "It's the squeaking wheel that gets the grease." That got publicity, all right. A couple from Maine, who had driven across America during the year, came back highly flattered. Every time they mentioned to new acquaintances that they were from Maine, they evoked a start of recognition: they were from the home state of that wonderful new Senator, Margaret Chase Smith!

Finally, during an interview with radio commentator Bob Trout, Margaret Smith put a brake on the wild predictions which were being made about her immediate future. The Republicans were still casting around for a ticket strong enough to push President Harry Truman out of office in the next election. Trout mentioned the rumors that she might go on from the Senate to the Vice-Presidency, or even—

"Suppose you woke up some morning and found yourself in the White House," he asked. "What would you do?"

"I'd go straight to Mrs. Truman and apologize," she replied crisply. "Then I'd go home."

It came as no surprise to anyone when, at the end of 1949, the Associated Press gave its award for "Woman of the Year" to Senator Margaret Chase Smith.

❧ 7 ❧

THE early summer of 1950 has been described as Margaret Smith's finest hour. It was in June of that year that she delivered in the Senate her "Declaration of Conscience," a document treasured not so much for its eloquence as for its timeliness; not so much for its originality as for its common sense. It was a plea by the Senate's lone woman to her 95 male colleagues to return that institution to the state in which its traditions had flowered. It was, in short, a breath of fresh air, blown into an institution whose atmosphere had turned dishonorable.

There is no doubt now that atmosphere was dishonorable. It was not that the Senate abounded in dishonorable men, but that a few who were unscrupulous, sparked by a mediocre but curiously twisted man, had capitalized on the nation's fears in order to seize the initiative. Because of recent history, the Senate's decent members were paralyzed not so much by fear (though there was that, too) but by uncertainty. In the unique Cold War which blighted the postwar world, the judgment of honest men was shaken in the mass of revelations, in the confused discussion of "patriotism," with its charges and countercharges, that swirled around them.

While the better Senators were devoting themselves to the business of legislation, Wisconsin's Republican Senator Joseph R. McCarthy was manufacturing headlines with his frantic efforts to uncover a Communist in government. As in most such cases, there was a basis of fact underlying the national hysteria. Soviet Russia had increased its espionage activity in the United States after the war. When Alger Hiss, a government official under Presidents Franklin D. Roosevelt and Harry Truman, was accused of being a part of the Soviet spy apparatus, many prominent Democrats rushed to his defense. Hiss' subsequent conviction for perjury was a blow to his defenders. Afraid of being charged with Communist sympathies, and unsure now of their own judgment, many prominent men in government became reluctant to speak out in defense of others who had been accused of "treason." Given a free hand, unscrupulous or fanatical men competed for national publicity and the attendant votes of the gullible by accusing almost everybody in sight of being "a Communist."

George Santayana, the philosopher and poet, once defined a fanatic as a man who redoubles his effort after he has forgotten his aim. Such was Senator McCarthy. Cloaked in the immunity from libel granted to Senators when they speak on the floor, he rose time after time to blacken the names of defenseless people by accusing them of treason and subversion without the faintest shred of evidence. Shocked by the Hiss case (in which McCarthy had played no part), Democratic Senators lacked the courage or the confidence to speak out against McCarthy. Republican leaders, hoping that their colleague from Wisconsin would uncover "another Hiss" if he kept at it, failed to restrain him. This hardly admirable state of affairs had badly tarnished the Senate, and had damaged America's prestige in the eyes of the civilized world.

Margaret Smith, though a popular figure throughout the

country, pulled little weight within the hierarchy of the Republican party. The Old Guard was not ready to accept a woman, especially one who did not fit into the mold of the traditional woman politician by being a "nice, pleasant soul anxious to please her betters." On the other hand, she shattered another popular picture of her sex: in an institution noted for its wordiness, she was distinguished by her ability to hold her tongue. She had yet to make a major speech in the Senate. And, when the Senate Republican Policy Committee (of which she was a member) met with the House Republican Policy Committee to draft a statement of their party's policy in the coming elections, she rebelled at the 2,500-word statement they produced. Upon her suggestion, and with the approval of the Republican National Committee, party leaders released a 99-word summary of their longer statement.

Now she was puzzled and disturbed by the unpleasant atmosphere around her in the Senate. Once, when asked by a reporter about McCarthyism, at a time when most Senators refused to discuss their colleague because of his attack on Senator Millard Tydings (who had displeased him), Margaret Smith did not evade the question.

"What is McCarthyism?" she repeated. "A lot of personal publicity for Senator McCarthy, I think."

Speaking of those days in later years, Margaret Smith has said: "Like everybody else I was hoping that Joe McCarthy would produce some solid evidence. Nobody wanted to cross him. You wondered when you were going to be called to task just because you'd said hello to the wrong person. It was so bad people were becoming almost deaf mutes."

Though, like most other Republicans, she believed the Democratic administration in Washington had been guilty of great carelessness in managing the country's security, she was appalled at the irresponsible attack McCarthy had made on so many earnest (if sometimes mistaken) Americans. She waited for her seniors in Congress to take action against McCarthy. Nothing happened.

"I've just about had it," she said one day to her administrative assistant, Bill Lewis.

Shortly afterward she boarded the little subway that shuttled back and forth between the Senate Office Building and the Capitol. Senator McCarthy took a seat beside her. One of McCarthy's assets was his agreeableness; many reporters and politicians had been won over to his side because he was "a nice guy." But Margaret Smith was not exchanging pleasantries that day.

"I'm going to make a speech, Joe," she told him. "And you're not going to like it."

"Be careful, Margaret," McCarthy replied, half seriously and half jokingly. "You know, you might lose Wisconsin's votes for Vice-President."

She did not rush hastily into battle. For six weeks, off and on, she thought about what she would say. She talked over her plans with men she trusted. Among them was Vermont's Republican Senator, George D. Aiken. Surprised at her determination, Aiken nevertheless encouraged her. She contacted five other Republicans who did not seem to her to be tied to the arch-conservatives who led the party. They were Charles Toby of New Hampshire, Irving Ives of New York, Edward Thye of Minnesota, Robert Hendrickson of New Jersey and Wayne Morse (who later became a Democrat) of Oregon. None of them disappointed her. Joined by Aiken, these five agreed to sign the "declaration" which she had prepared.

On June 1, she appeared in the green-carpeted, crescent-shaped Senate Chamber, her gray hair immaculately done, looking cool yet determined in her aquamarine silk suit; the fresh red rose, as always, sparkled on her lapel. Word had gotten around that she was to make her first important speech in the Senate, and a large crowd was on hand. She took her place at her desk, on the Republican side of the narrow center aisle. Just behind her sat the burly Senator from Wisconsin, Joe McCarthy.

When she rose to speak, other Senators on both sides of the aisle moved closer to hear her. Her voice wasn't loud, but it was clear and firm. As she spoke she occasionally looked down at the cards she held in her hands.

"I would like to speak briefly and simply about a serious national condition," she began. "It is a national feeling of fear and frustration that could result in national suicide and the end of everything that we Americans hold dear. It is a condition that comes from the lack of effective leadership in either the legislative branch or the executive branch of our government."

As McCarthy alternately scowled and placed his head in his hand, Margaret Smith lashed out at the tactics which had caused the Senate, once the most admired deliberative body in the world, to be "debased to the level of a forum of hate and character assassination sheltered by the shield of Congressional immunity."

Never mentioning McCarthy, or the party leaders who had privately encouraged him while publicly keeping their distance from his methods, Margaret Smith suggested that "it is high time for the United States Senate and its members to do some soul-searching. . . . It is high time that we remembered that the Constitution, as amended, speaks not only of freedom of speech but also of trial by jury instead of trial by accusation."

With simple force she pointed out that the very men who were shouting the loudest about their "Americanism" were those who were ignoring at the same time some of the basic principles of Americanism. She vigorously defended every

American's right to criticize, to think independently and to hold unpopular beliefs.

"Who of us doesn't?" she asked the great hushed chamber. "Otherwise none of us could call our souls our own. Otherwise thought control would have set in. The American people are sick and tired of being afraid to speak their minds lest they be smeared as 'Communists' or 'Fascists' by their opponents. Freedom of speech is not what it used to be in America. It has been so abused by some that it is not exercised by others."

Shifting her attack to the Democratic administration, she said that the American people were not only sick of seeing innocent people smeared, but they were also sick of seeing the guilty whitewashed. She said that the administration's failure to vigorously combat internal subversion had caused the public to lose confidence in it, and led to "the confusion and suspicions that are bred in the United States Senate to spread like cancerous tentacles." She asserted her belief that the Truman administration was a burden on the country.

"Yet to displace it with a Republican regime embracing a philosophy that lacks political integrity or intellectual honesty would prove equally disastrous to this nation. The nation sorely needs a Republican victory. But I don't want to see the Republican party ride to political victory on the Four Horsemen of Calumny—Fear, Ignorance, Bigotry and Smear."

In closing, she said: "As an American, I want to see our nation recapture the strength and unity it once had when we fought the enemy instead of ourselves." She then read the brief "Declaration of Conscience," signed by the six Republicans she had spoken to earlier. They joined her in saying that it was time "we stopped being tools and victims of totalitarian techniques—techniques that, if continued here unchecked, will surely end what we have come to cherish as the American way of life."

When she sat down it was as if, with one ringing blow, she had cleared the atmosphere of the venerable chamber. Things happened that hadn't happened there in a long time. McCarthy, who had promised to "ask her some very pointed questions after the speech," got up and, his face grimly dark, left the Capitol without saying a word. Where, only a few short minutes before, the most powerful men in the country would have hesitated before consorting with those who had attacked McCarthy, her colleagues now came over to congratulate her. New York's Senator Herbert Lehman told reporters that "she said things which had to be said and should have been said a long time ago."

Maryland's Senator Millard Tydings called for a new word: "Stateswomanship." And Missouri's Democratic Senator Stuart Symington said: "Senator Smith represents just about all that is best today in American public life—even if she is a Republican."

"I didn't do it for approval or disapproval," Margaret Smith said. "I just thought it had to be done. It's one of the things I've felt strongly about."

Letters poured in from all over the country, running about eight to one in her favor. She answered them all, sending thanks to those who agreed with her, and politely acknowledging the others with an observation that "America is big enough and great enough to include people of various opinions." Editorial comment in the nation's newspapers was generally favorable. Margaret Smith had, in her country's hour of deep trouble, stepped in with a brave and independent gesture.

But she had not yet heard from Senator Joseph R. McCarthy.

❧ 8 ❧

It is difficult from this distance to appreciate the climate of fear which then prevailed in political, academic and scientific America. To speak out against Joseph McCarthy and his followers, or the views they held sacred, was to invite certain retaliation; the livelihood and reputations of many Americans were jeopardized or destroyed because of their insistence on what should have been their inviolate right to freedom of speech. Margaret Chase Smith was about to undergo her trial by fire.

McCarthy remained silent for less than twenty-four hours after her speech. Then he released a snarling, sarcastic statement in which he referred to Margaret Smith and the Senators who had signed her "Declaration of Conscience" as "Snow White and the Six Dwarfs." Names could not hurt Margaret Smith, but McCarthy's sticks and stones were still to come.

The Wisconsin Senator bided his time through the remainder of that session. Margaret Smith came under attack from his followers from time to time, but McCarthy first turned his attention to Maryland's Senator Millard Tydings, who had also affronted him, and who was especially vulnerable now because he was running for re-election. Moving into Maryland, McCarthy's followers waged such a vicious campaign while insuring Tydings' defeat that it became the subject of a later Senate investigation. With Tydings disposed of and the 1951 session of Congress now underway, McCarthy once more turned his attention to Margaret Smith.

After entering the Senate she had been appointed to the Senate Expenditures Committee (of which Harry Truman had been chairman when he was a Senator before World War Two); through this post she had become a member of that committee's key investigating subcommittee. Arkansas' Democratic Senator John McClellan was now the committee chairman because his party controlled the Senate, but Joe McCarthy was the committee's senior Republican member and so had the right to name the other Republicans to its subcommittees. When McCarthy passed around a memorandum designating the Republican assignments for the new session, Margaret Smith's name had been removed from the investigations subcommittee and placed on the less-important reorganization subcommittee. Her place on the investigations panel was filled by a freshman Senator from California named Richard M. Nixon.

The next morning eight members of the parent Expenditures Committee met in a closed session. Margaret Smith immediately stood up and challenged McCarthy's right to remove her from the subcommittee in favor of a Senator who was her junior. Senator McClellan evaded her demand for a ruling by claiming that it was McCarthy's right to assign his own members. She carried the battle to the Wisconsin Senator.

"Nobody here is fooling anybody else," she fumed. "I was bumped from that subcommittee."

McCarthy tried to calm the lady, explaining that he simply was anxious to have Nixon, who had helped to destroy Alger Hiss, serve on the investigations subcommittee because of his experience. "He did a tremendous job on the House Un-American Activities Committee," McCarthy said.

Margaret Smith was ready for him. "Joe, I was making investigations in the House three years before you and Senator Nixon got to Washington!"

But the change had been made. Later McCarthy denied to reporters that her "Declaration of Conscience" in the previous session had had anything to do with the change of assignments. "I'm surprised there should be such a fuss over a routine matter," he said blandly. "Nixon, like everybody else, wanted to be on the investigations subcommittee, and a choice had to be made. But it's not right to say that Margaret was bumped. She was promoted to another highly important job."

Another blow fell almost immediately: she lost her place on the Republican Policy Committee to Senator Brewster, her old sparring partner from Maine. She was less bitter toward McCarthy, from whom she expected retaliation, than she was toward Senator Taft and the other Republican leaders; these changes could have been made only with their tacit consent. She had not always supported Taft's policies, of course; in a recent Republican statement which asked for the removal of Truman's Secretary of State, Dean Acheson, she had disassociated herself from the Republicans' savage attack and voted with the Democrats. But she had done several important favors for Taft, too, particularly on the proposed Lucas Amendment to the Taft-Hartley Labor Act. This amendment would have removed the injunction clause, which Taft had felt was vital to the bill's effectiveness. Had she voted for the amendment, it would have brought about a tie, and Vice-President Barkley (who was entitled to vote in the event of a tie in the Senate) would have ensured the amendment's passage. Instead, she bowed to Taft's plea and her vote defeated the amendment, 46–44. On another occasion she had deserted the other Republican liberals and cast her vote for Taft as chairman of the Senate Republican Policy Committee. Now she knew (and McCarthy had admitted it to her) that it was with the consent of Taft that she had been removed from this committee.

Again the press seemed solidly on Margaret Smith's side. "She could pursue a continuous crusade against McCarthyism only at the risk of party ostracism which would render it ineffective," *The Nation* said in an editorial. "So instead she has let the declaration ferment in the voters' consciences while she tries to be the best Senator and Republican she knows how to be."

Her colleagues in the Senate also said a good word for her in this dark moment. Democratic Senator Harry Byrd of Virginia made a public statement praising her economic views (implying that nobody who agreed with *his* orthodox economics could possibly be a Communist sympathizer), while that arch-conservative, Pat McCarran of Nevada, bestowed on her his own certificate of patriotism: "I would like very much to have her as a member of my committee investigating subversives."

The battle was to flare up at intervals for several years. There is no need here to go into all the sordid details of that period of the Senate's history, but a few of the highlights which marked one Senator's struggle against the "no-nothings" may prove instructive.

Though Margaret Smith did not carry on a personal vendetta against McCarthy (suggesting a more bipartisan policy by the administration, she asked President Truman to consult "such critical Republicans as Senators Joseph R. McCarthy and William F. Knowland before making decisions on affairs of state"), she remained alert for any outbreaks of "demagoguery." When McCarthy launched a vicious and unwarranted attack on General George C. Marshall, a respected soldier and statesman, Margaret Smith had her "Declaration of Conscience" re-inserted in the *Congressional Record,* appending the remark that it was now more applicable than ever before. And, speaking in Houlton, Maine, that fall, she called for a return to the traditional initiative for which Americans used to be known.

"When we accept the statements and proposals of demagogues," she said, "because we are too lazy to think and test their statements we can blame no one but ourselves for subsequent events. . . . We are closer to surrending our freedom than most of us are willing to recognize or admit."

By this time Margaret Smith was a member of a Senate committee which had been appointed to investigate the scandals connected with the defeat in Maryland of Senator Millard Tydings. McCarthy, of course, had ridiculed the investigation. But when Senator Taft agreed with him, Margaret Smith neatly turned the tables.

Taft had tried to brush off the Maryland election scandal with the comment that it was nothing compared to what had happened in Ohio, when he had run for re-election in 1950. Margaret Smith heard him through, then told the subcommittee:

"If this is so, perhaps we had better look into the Ohio elections too."

Taft was furious, especially because the investigation had not been cleared with him. Though his supporters later claimed that Taft had had nothing to do with the anti-Catholic whispering which had been a part of the campaign waged for him in Ohio (comparable to the fraudulent photographs which were supposed to link Tydings with Communists in the Maryland campaign) he was not anxious to have these charges investigated.

The investigation proved that Taft's bitter charges about the millions poured into his opponent's campaign were hogwash; Taft's own campaign had cost a great deal more. The most dramatic moment of the investigation came when Margaret Smith challenged Taft's campaign statement that linked the C.I.O. with Communism. In the presence of Willis B. Gradison, who had managed Taft's campaign, she read excerpts from a speech Taft had made at Cleveland. There the Ohio Senator had said that the C.I.O.'s Political Action Committee was conceived and nurtured by Communists.

"Wouldn't you say that this is a pretty extravagant statement you couldn't back up with facts?" she asked Gradison.

"I certainly couldn't back it up," Gradison said. "I have no doubt the Senator at least attempted to back it up."

Under questioning by Margaret Smith and the rest of the committee, Gradison admitted that he would not contend the C.I.O.-P.A.C. was controlled or dominated by Communists. It was, he said, only "infiltrated." He also softened his earlier testimony that Communist leader "Gus Hall blueprinted the campaign against Taft." He admitted that it would have been better to say simply that the Communists opposed Taft. Later Taft's treasurer claimed that he had kept no records of the money he gave in 1950 to such groups as the Advertising Committee for Taft and the Physicians' Committee for Taft. The investigations brought no charges against anybody.

The skirmishes went on. In 1952, when a move was brought by Connecticut's Senator William Benton to expel McCarthy from the Senate on the grounds that he had lied to that body, Margaret Smith and McCarthy clashed again. She was a member of a Senate subcommittee which had been given the task of investigating McCarthy. The Great Investigator was outraged at being investigated. He assailed the subcommittee and claimed that its members "were guilty of stealing just as clearly as though they engaged in picking the pockets of the taxpayers."

Margaret Smith, like the other Senators on the subcommittee, resented being called a thief. The entire Senate was asked to display its confidence in the subcommittee. Margaret Smith spoke to the Senate, quietly but firmly, tearing McCarthy's statement to shreds. As she continued her attack, a reporter in the press gallery could be heard to murmur: "She has guts!"

McCarthy, foreseeing that the Senate would vote its confidence in the subcommittee, tried to take the sting out of its action by announcing that if he were able to be there he too would give the subcommittee a vote of confidence; unfortunately, he had a pressing engagement elsewhere.

Though the very clannishness of the Senate prevented its various members from expelling one of their own, no matter how dangerous or obnoxious they found him to be (McCarthy was eventually "censured" in 1954, not for having committed outrages against the American public but for having obstructed the investigation of himself), the running battle continued. In 1953, when the Democratic members of McCarthy's investigating subcommittee resigned in disgust, McCarthy sought to issue reports in the entire subcommittee's name while the Senate was in recess. It was Margaret Smith who led the fight that prevented him from doing this.

The campaign against Margaret Smith reached its peak of absurdity in 1952 when a pair of reporters named Jack Lait and Lee Mortimer wrote a book called *U. S. A. Confidential*. Though dwelling on sin in its various sensational manifestations (chiefly sex) the book found time to link Margaret Smith to the Communist Conspiracy in the United States:

Maine's other phenomenon is Margaret Chase Smith, sole female U. S. Senator. The last time we were in Washington she was making one of her boneheaded speeches. A Senate doorman couldn't stand it any longer. When she reached the high point of her peroration, he sniffed and remarked about the lone female, "There's too many women in the Senate!"

She is a lesson in why women should not be in politics. When men argue matters of high policy they usually forget their grudges at the door. She takes every opposing speech as a personal affront and lies awake nights scheming how to "get even." She is sincere—but a dame—and she reacts to all situations as a woman scorned, not as a representative of the people. She is under the influence of the coterie of left-wing writers and reporters who dominate Washington and they praise her so assiduously she believes it.

Lait and Mortimer went on to claim that Margaret Smith was "pals" with a woman they described as a "security risk." They also claimed that she was a "left-wing apologist" and a "stunted visionary." Perhaps worst of all, as if they had intended to get under her skin, they referred to her as "Maggie." When the book was published and became a best seller, she sued the authors for one million dollars.

In her suit, which charged that they had brought her into "scandal as an associate of and sympathizer with Communists," her attorneys asked Lait and Mortimer to "specify the nights on which she lay awake scheming how to get even." They also asked the authors to specify the date on which they were in Washington to hear her speak, and to supply the name of the Senate doorman who remarked that there were too many women in the Senate. In reply, the authors' lawyer said that her questions were "specious," and he put her through an extensive pre-trial examination in which he attempted to find out where she deviated from McCarthy's beliefs. The suit lingered for four years, and was finally scheduled to come before Federal Judge Edward J. Dimmock in New York City. According to Richard H. Wels, Margaret Smith's attorney, both Estes Kefauver, Democratic Senator from Tennessee, and California's William F. Knowland, Republican leader in the Senate, were scheduled to testify in her behalf. Suddenly, Mortimer and his publisher (Lait had died) came to the conclusion that Margaret Smith was not a "Communist sympathizer" after all. They agreed to pay her $15,000 in damages, and pay for advertisements which appeared in several Maine newspapers. The advertisements said, in part:

> More thorough investigation since the publication of the book has convinced Lee Mortimer, the estate of Jack Lait and Crown Publishers, Inc., that the statements concerning Senator Margaret Chase Smith were mistaken and should not have been made.
>
> Senator Smith enjoys an excellent and enviable reputation.
>
> Nothing in the book was meant to reflect on the patriotism, honesty, morality or good citizenship of Senator Smith, nor was anything meant to say or imply that she was an apologist for or a sympathizer with Communists or Reds.
>
> We regret very much these mistaken statements concerning Senator Smith. We are now convinced that they were untrue, although made unintentionally.
>
> In fairness to Senator Smith we are happy to make these corrections.

∾ 9 ∾

But these wrangling affairs make headlines, not good legislators. It was Margaret Smith's determination to be a good
Senator, just as she had been a valuable Representative. "I
don't have any family, so my job is pretty much my life,"
she once said. She was soon distinguished in the Senate (a
hard-working unit, despite its reputation for monkey business) by her capacity for hard work.

"She's unbelievably meticulous," one fellow Senator said
of her. "She comes in with a good case or she doesn't come
in at all. She's a very gracious woman, and she doesn't like
to pick a fight, but the questions she asks can be very sharp.
God help the man who gives her a smart answer. Give her
a horsey answer and she'll fly all over you."

When she was a member of the special subcommittee
investigating the McCarthy-engineered smear of Senator
Tydings in the 1950 Maryland election, she was given credit
for the fact that any report was ever issued. "We were having plenty of trouble trying to get together on a report," one
of the subcommittee members said. "So little Margaret just
dug her heels into the ground and told us either we all got
together on a report by May first or she would come out alone

with her own. We got out a report." It attacked McCarthy and his methods.

She considered her votes carefully, and cast them without regard to party label. It became fashionable to refer to her as a "liberal," a term to which she objected. "I don't think people know what they mean sometimes when they use that word," she said. "I'm an independent, and I think that's what my record really shows."

But independence is an ugly word to party regulars (of whatever party), who demand close, unthinking obedience to the line put out by their leaders. In 1952 many of the Republican leaders favored Senator Robert A. Taft as the man best fitted to turn out the Democratic administrations which had ruled Washington since 1932. Margaret Smith had been invited to appear at a clambake in 1951 to kick off Taft's campaign for the Republican Presidential nomination (the clambake was sponsored by Maine's Senator Owen Brewster, who hoped to become the Vice-Presidential candidate on a Taft ticket). Politically she has always taken a more moderate line, closer to that of Dwight D. Eisenhower than to those of the extreme of either party. She sent her regrets to the sponsors of the clambake, pleading that her duties in the Senate that day would make it impossible for her to attend. It has long been thought to be a fetish with her that she refuses to miss a Senate roll call for even the most trivial issues. Her record for always being present, however, has other uses than simply that of impressing the home folks that she takes her job seriously. It comes in very handy as an excuse when invitations arrive that she would just as soon decline. Who can quarrel with a lady's devotion to duty?

It was about the same time (1951) that a serious drive got underway to nominate General Eisenhower for the Presidency. The Far Right was active in trying to prevent his nomination. From the mills of the hate-peddlers came pamphlets and leaflets, spewing forth the same filth which is flung at every object of their wrath. Eisenhower was described as a Communist dupe, a Russian agent (how familiar this junk is to readers of the John Birch Society's literature!), a tool of "Jewish Conspirators" and a moral horror. These pamphlets, drifting in from the West, were picked up and distributed by the Maine State Republican Committee. Taft's sponsors in Maine took a hand in the pamphlets' distribution. One of the sections of the pamphlet which endeared it to the Maine "Old Guard" was a prediction that Margaret Smith would be among the "Republican renegades" likely to support the "New Deal-Communist plot" behind Eisenhower.

Margaret Smith fought back. Speaking to her Maine constituents on a radio program, she said: "I was shocked to find that copies of this smear pamphlet had been mailed out by headquarters of the Maine Republican State Committee to members of the State Committee. The mailing of such literature certainly violated the rule of a strict hands-off policy on candidates before the nomination.

"And certainly funds of the Republican State Committee could be put to more effective use in the interest of the Republican Party to build it up than to mail out such smear literature that tries to tear down a great American, General Dwight D. Eisenhower."

State Committee members seemed astonished that anyone could take offense at such "educational material." One member replied that Margaret Smith must be opposed to free speech. Brewster's followers said that Margaret Smith was probably trying to promote Eisenhower's candidacy. She reminded her critics that she had not yet come out for *anybody* as the Republican Presidential candidate.

"To interpret my objection to smear literature as being the opening gun for a personal drive for General Eisenhower is absurd," she said. "It is puzzling unless those who have made such misinterpretations consider the California smear sheet to be pro-Taft (since it is anti-Eisenhower as well as anti-Smith) and the distributors of that sheet to be promoters of the Presidential candidacy of Senator Taft."

Continuing her attack against dirty campaign literature, she questioned Republican National Chairman Guy Gabrielson, who was appearing before the Senate Elections Subcommittee, to explain how campaigns could be made less dirty. She brought up the case of the smear pamphlets. Gabrielson, a devoted follower of Taft, replied that the National Committee could not be interested in a candidate until he had been nominated by the party. Only after extensive questioning did he admit the pamphlets in question were "silly." Later Taft himself disavowed them when he announced his candidacy.

As summer approached in 1952 and the two major political parties prepared to nominate their Presidential candidates, Margaret Smith's name was frequently mentioned for the Republican Vice-Presidential spot. Such consideration for a woman was not unprecedented. Nellie Tayloe Ross, who had been the first woman governor in the United States (having been elected in Wyoming to succeed her husband after he had died in office), was suggested for the Vice-Presidency in 1928. At the Democratic Convention that year she received 28 votes. Though she never became Vice-President, she got to Washington anyway, being appointed the first woman director of the United States Mint. She served in that post for many years.

Margaret Smith did not get that close to the nomination. Though her candidacy was endorsed by the National Federation of Business and Professional Women's Clubs, representing 150,000 women, and though Clare Boothe Luce made a nice speech in her behalf at the Republican Convention, she never really had a chance—especially after Eisenhower got the Presidential nomination. As a sop to the right-wingers, the Eisenhower faction had to take Richard M. Nixon in the Vice-Presidential slot to reaffirm party unity. But, as Mrs. Luce revealed after her speech, Margaret Smith already had told her that she was not interested in the nomination. "I have a job to do here in the Senate," Margaret Smith had said.

In fact, her name, so prominently mentioned before the convention, was not among the speakers when the convention itself got underway. Drew Pearson, in his syndicated column, reported that Senator McCarthy had been behind the move which kept her from convention prominence. Originally she had been invited by House Speaker Joseph Martin, a Republican leader, to be a prominent speaker at the Republican Convention in Chicago. She was allotted twenty-five minutes to speak. Later this was chopped to fifteen minutes. Finally, Martin called her back to tell her that it had been decided that she could speak for only five minutes.

"And you'll have to represent a minority," Martin said.

"What do you mean, a minority?" Margaret Smith asked. "Are you dividing the party up into the Irish and Greeks and Jews and Negroes?"

"No," Martin said. "You represent the women."

"Under the circumstances," she said, "you can give the five minutes to somebody else."

Margaret Smith never publicly resented being pushed aside at the convention, but she has forcefully stated her opposition to the method of selecting Presidential and Vice-Presidential candidates. "Because candidates are picked in the 'smoked-filled' rooms by party bosses," she has said, "it is practically impossible for a woman to have a chance to be considered, much less to be nominated. And yet the majority of voters in this country are women." (She has, as we shall see, made proposals for a change in both the nomination of candidates and the Presidential elections themselves.)

The Eisenhower sweep in the 1952 elections brought a Republican majority into the Senate and a couple of fine committee assignments for Margaret Smith. Already on the Government Operations Committee, she received appointments to the Armed Services Committee (her experience on the House Armed Services Committee, and her 1950 commission as a Lt. Colonel in the Air Force Reserve were two of her outstanding qualifications for this post) and the Appropriations Committee. The Senate, like the House, is run by committees, and her appointment to two of the more powerful ones enhanced her value to her constituents, and to the Senate as well.

The Armed Services Committee gave her a platform from which she could be of value to the State of Maine. The military is one of the five top industries in Maine, which makes the assignment of extra projects there of vital interest to its people. The Armed Services Committee is an excellent place for a Senator who wants to do something for his constituents (as, of course, they all do). A committee can approve new projects, or it can squash them. William S. White, in his book *Citadel,* has described the individualistic ways in which members of powerful committees can affect legislation. He tells of Tom Connally, the colorful Senator from Texas, who was chairman of the Foreign Relations Committee. When California's Senator Knowland pressed Connally to act on a Knowland proposal which the foreign policy leaders considered unwise, Connally cried from the Senate floor in mock humility:

"I assure the Senator from California that his matter will have in the Foreign Relations Committee *exactly* the consideration that it so richly deserves." Here Connally looked up at the press gallery, grinned and passed his index finger across his throat like the blade of a knife.

While not so dramatic, Margaret Smith has done her job in committee well. One of her first important assignments was that of chairman of an Armed Services Subcommittee investigating ammunition shortages during the Korean war. The investigation, which took place in 1953, was unusually thorough. Grave mistakes were found to have been made.

"It is apparent," she said in a preliminary statement, "that there has been much red tape which was not effectively dealt with by Army officials ... evidence that we were trying to fight a war abroad and maintain a semblance of peace at home. The apparent result of this was that the ammunition program did not receive the driving force it deserved."

The final report of her subcommittee rendered a blistering judgment against the Truman administration, under which the war had been fought. A majority report, signed by Republicans Margaret Smith, Robert C. Hendrickson of New Jersey, John Sherman Cooper of Kentucky, and Democrat Harry Byrd of Virginia, said that the ammunition shortage had caused "needless loss of American lives" in Korea. Although responsibility could not be pinpointed, the report said that President Truman, several members of his Cabinet, his Joint Chiefs of Staff and the National Security Council shared in miscalculating "the aggressive designs of International Communism."

There were other marks of her progress in the Senate. She also became chairman of a subcommittee which dealt efficiently with President Eisenhower's reorganization bill for the new Department of Health, Education and Welfare, and she was reappointed to the Senate Republican Policy Committee, from which she had been bumped after her "Declaration of Conscience" speech. Writing in *The Christian Science Monitor* in July, 1953, Josephine Ripley praised Margaret Smith's contributions to committee work:

She quickly established a reputation for asking good questions and for being able to keep things under control, no small accomplishment when flanked by such political stars as Senator Byrd of Virginia and Senator Kefauver of Tennessee. . . . Back of Senator Smith's success in the Senate are two outstanding characteristics—a ladylike poise and a determined jaw. This has been an effective combination. It has won the respect of her colleagues on both counts—as a legislator who conducts herself with dignity and poise and who can stand up for her rights when the occasion demands it.

In Washington she had now been accorded the recognition she deserved. One incident must have been particularly gratifying. In polls of the press and political scientists she was voted among the ten top Senators; Joe McCarthy finished dead last.

❧ 10 ❧

Margaret Smith, though she has often outraged the Far
Right on matters pertaining to labor, civil rights and other
social problems, has from the first displayed a "hardness"
toward Communists, foreign or domestic, to satisfy the most
eminent patriot. Indeed few of the professional Red-baiters
have gone so far in this crusade. The most superficial review
of her record on this question must convince the impartial
observer that it was not Margaret Smith's "sympathy with
Reds" which was behind the bitter attacks on her, but her
concern for the rights of the American individual.

Her thinking on Communism is not particularly brilliant,
nor particularly original. It can best be described as a reli-
ance on the simple solution, and can best be illustrated with
several of her actions in Congress during 1953 and 1954. The
Korean war had first alerted the American public to the
menace of Red China. Before this, Russia had been considered the prime enemy, but the Chinese troops which
poured across the Yalu River and dealt the United Nations
forces (chiefly United States troops) such heavy blows in
Korea aroused natural and intense anger in this country;
when President Truman and UN leaders decided to try to
contain the war within the boundaries of Korea, and not hit

the Chinese mainland in retaliation, this great American anger turned to frustration. A truce was signed in 1953, but the frustration lingered.

When Red China continued to make threatening noises, and the United States Government exercised a good deal of restraint in its answers, Margaret Smith thought we had been pushed around long enough. Instead of speaking from the Senate floor, she chose to launch her attack in the column she was writing five days a week (and which she finally abandoned because of the press of other duties later in 1953). Perhaps, like many writers, Margaret Smith had finally run out of ideas for her column. At any rate, she made threatening noises of her own, going far beyond what most other responsible Americans were prepared to say at the time.

"If the current negotiations don't produce peace but do break down and the war is resumed," she wrote, "then drop the atomic bomb on these barbarians who obviously in their past atrocities have proved that they have no concept of a desire for decency."

Reminding her readers that the Chinese Reds, unwilling to listen to reason, were bent on destroying us, she said that we had no choice but to destroy them first. Hurling anathema like a medieval pope, she continued:

"We have tried everything else. Maybe the atomic bomb will bring the Red barbarians to their senses as it did the Japanese."

She anticipated some moral opposition to her modest proposal. "I know that some will protest that the atomic bomb is an immoral weapon. I agree that it is. But so are all other man-killing weapons of war. War itself is immoral because it is nothing less than organized murder. Yet when we are attacked we do not refuse to fight simply because we know that war is immoral.

"Instead we not only stand up and defend ourselves from

being murdered, but like the policeman on the street we act to stop the murderers from killing other people. Like the policeman who shoots and kills a murderer who is shooting at him, so do we in war shoot and kill the murderers who shoot at us, not only to kill us individually but our country.

"When will we learn that you don't stop the Red murderers by merely playing tiddly-winks with them?"

The following March she turned her attention to the home-grown Reds. She introduced the first bill ever proposed in the Senate to outlaw the Communist party in this country. Her attack was mounted as spiritedly as before. Her bill was based, she said, on the fact that the Communist party is not a political party, but an instrument of Soviet Russia, determined to overthrow our government by violence and subversion.

"Here is not a matter of political freedom but of criminal action," she said. "The Communist party is professionally engaged in treason, certainly a crime worse than gambling, vice and the other actions covered by the criminal statutes."

She found an inconsistency in the government's position, and pounced on it: a Communist is barred from insignificant positions in government offices, but at the same time, as a member of a political party, he can run for Congress or the Presidency itself.

"One principal objection advanced against outlawing the Communist party is the contention that to do so would drive them underground and therefore make it more difficult to identify members and expose them. This argument is not impressive. We know that the Communist party, certainly the dangerous part, is underground now. It could hardly be driven further underground.

"We recognize that murder of an individual human being is a crime—and make it a crime punishable by death or life imprisonment. We must make Communist party membership a crime before it is too late—before our nation has been murdered by Communists."

Though the bill was not passed, Margaret Smith was now as disliked in Moscow as she was among certain segments of the American Right. (In 1955, when she and Representative Frances Bolton introduced a somewhat different bill to Congress, suggesting that the rose be adopted as the national flower, the Soviet armed forces newspaper, *Red Star,* took the opportunity to denounce Margaret Smith as "a military Amazon who hides behind bouquets of roses.") Meanwhile, the American Right was attempting a more direct assault upon her. Margaret Smith's first six-year term in the Senate expired in 1954, and she was faced with another heated battle. Before she met the Democratic nominee in the election, she had to dispose of the opposition from within her own party.

She knew well in advance that she would be in for a fight. It was a peculiar situation because on the surface there was no opponent she could single out and strike back at; no professional politician within Maine's Republican party would be foolish enough to run against her, for her popularity with the people throughout the state was now enormous. In the cities and small towns there were volunteers (people who ordinarily never thought of pitching in to help during an election campaign) ready to rally to Margaret Smith. But where was the opposition? In neither the Republican nor the Democratic party was an opponent in sight.

The Old Guard dug deep, but they came up with an opponent. He was Robert L. Jones, a man whose qualifications as a replacement for Margaret Smith apparently began and ended with his sympathy for Senator McCarthy, and his experience as an aide to one of the Senate's leading conservatives, Senator William Jenner of Indiana. A suspicion that

Jones was in the race more to discredit Margaret Smith than to win a Senate seat (he actually had no chance) was confirmed when it was revealed that much of his campaign funds came from Texas oil millionaires—many of whom have been, and are, active in Far Right movements.

Margaret Smith was furious. "Those rich Texans not only want to keep their money through oil depletion allowances," she told a friend, "and make the rest of us pay extra taxes, but they also send their money all over the country to defeat the Senators who don't agree with them. They want to make the Senate of the United States a rubber stamp for Texas."

It was a subject she went into at length later on. But for now she had a primary battle to fight. Jones himself proved to be a weak opponent, and Margaret Smith paid him such little heed that she mentioned his name only twice during the campaign. As usual, she stuck to her record. Some of Jones' supporters, however, used questionable tactics in an effort to beef up his campaign. One story was circulated to the effect that Margaret Smith was in poor health. The same kind of anti-Semitic literature that had been used against Eisenhower three years before (linking the candidate with sinister Jewish interests) was introduced into Maine. There are many skilled politicians who advocate a rough campaign. Murray Chotiner, who handled some of the campaigns of Richard M. Nixon, once outlined his theory of successful campaigning:

"If you do not deflate the opposition candidate before your own campaign gets started, the odds are that you are going to be doomed to defeat. . . . The American people . . . vote against a candidate, against a party, or against an issue, rather than for a candidate or an issue or a party."

There are different ways in which a victim responds to such a campaign. Mrs. Edith Green, who was running for the House of Representatives in Oregon's Third Congressional District, came up against an opponent who was determined to bring her down by any means. He charged her with being "a puppet and mouthpiece of Eastern labor racketeers." Mrs. Green, on the theory that the best defense is a good offense, immediately challenged her opponent to a television debate. He, of course, declined. She turned this to her advantage by playing a tape of his offensive speech on a program of her own. Then she sent him a check for his services (at union rates) as a recorded television performer.

Margaret Smith responded to smear tactics less dramatically, but with equally good effect. "I always use the same technique," she said. "I say what I'm for, rather than what I'm against."

Although Jones apparently had Joe McCarthy's support at the beginning of the campaign, the Wisconsin Senator soon sensed he hadn't the ghost of a chance and left his protégé on his own. Jones, feeling little public enthusiasm for McCarthy around him, denied he was "McCarthy's boy." He did hasten to add: "But I admire the Senator from Wisconsin," and said that a victory for his side in Maine would be "a signal of the rebirth of Americanism and our opposition to internationalism."

Margaret Smith described the situation simply: "My opponent has Senator McCarthy's support, and I am sure the Senator would be very happy to see me defeated."

But the Wisconsin Senator deserted the sinking ship several months before the primary ended. Sherman Adams, the special assistant to President Eisenhower, made a personal appeal to Maine's Republican leaders to support Margaret Smith. And the final primary voting, which the experts predicted would go in her favor by a 3–1 margin, turned into a catastrophe for Jones when she piled up 96,457 votes to Jones' 19,336, a margin of almost 5–1. She won 623 of

Maine's 626 voting precincts. And so ended the celebrated battle between Smith and Jones.

In the September election Margaret Smith faced an equally inexperienced but far different kind of foe. For many years the Democratic party in Maine had languished; it won so seldom that Maine was, almost in the old Southern sense, a one-party state. In the spring of 1954 the Democrats were so disorganized they weren't sure they could find enough volunteers to fill out a slate against the Republicans. A couple of meetings were hastily called in Augusta to discuss possible candidates; only five Democrats showed up at the first meeting, twelve at the second. But among those at the second meeting was Edmund S. Muskie, a lawyer from Waterville and a promising young politician. Muskie, it was decided, would run for governor which, in view of the Democrats' lack of candidates, was not a surprise. What was a surprise, especially to the man involved, was the designation of Professor Paul A. Fullam to run against Margaret Smith.

Fullam, a history professor at Colby College, had accompanied Muskie to Augusta simply for the ride. Interested in political theory, he had never thought of trying for public office. But after being selected as a candidate for the Senate, and having found that Colby's board of trustees had no objections to his candidacy, Fullam threw himself into the campaign as vigorously as any experienced politician.

What had appeared to be another Republican walkover soon became a desperate struggle as Maine's vigorous young Democrats pounded away at the GOP's record. Intelligent and well-informed, Fullam also turned out to be a persuasive speaker. Hard times had fallen upon the state. Republican Governor Burton M. Cross had outraged the potato growers of Aroostook County by his stand against price supports, and the textile workers by his failure to lure new industry (and thus new jobs) to Maine. The clam diggers were up in arms about the polluted state of the mud flats, and the sardine workers were in their usual depressed position.

"The people will have to lift themselves by their bootstraps," was Governor Cross' solution to hard times Down East. This seemed to many people the practical application of the Republicans' "Peace and Prosperity" campaign slogan, and they looked elsewhere for relief.

"Towns that had never held a Democratic meeting started calling state headquarters and asking, 'How do we hold a caucus?'" Muskie has recalled.

Vice-President Nixon visited Maine to tell the voters that the coming election (held nearly two months ahead of other state elections throughout America) was a test of the Eisenhower administration's popularity. Many Republicans, though they admitted that this time the Democratic candidates were a cut above their party's usual candidates in the state, still looked for a traditionally easy Republican victory. But, as the campaign swirled into its final hours, Margaret Smith took a different view of matters: she knew that the whole Republican slate was in danger.

On the evening before Election Day she appeared on a television program with other leading Republican candidates. Her parting word to the viewers was to watch a program on which she would appear alone later in the evening. It was there that, for the first time, she abandoned her usual emphasis on her own record and resorted to what many of her critics later claimed was the use of the very same underhanded tactics of which she accused the Far Right.

On her half-hour TV program she went after Professor Fullam. Reading occasionally from notes, nodding her head frequently for emphasis, she accused Fullam of lying about her during the campaign. Then, her eyes glinting with anger, she produced a sworn, notarized Republican nomination paper for her candidacy. She held it close before the camera, then pointed to the signature of Professor Paul A. Fullam. Then she signed off.

Whether this last-minute attack had helped her or not, she did better the next day than most of her Republican running mates. Governor Cross went down to defeat before young Muskie, the first time in Maine's modern political history that a Republican governor had been defeated in his try for a second term. Margaret Smith held a clear lead over Fullam, polling 144,530 votes to the professor's 102,075. It was, however, something of a setback, for she polled only 58 percent of the total vote, compared with the 71 percent she had polled in 1948. She was now assured of another six years in the Senate.

The campaign itself had a tragic aftermath. Fullam, though too late, angrily replied to Margaret Smith's zero-hour TV program. He explained that, when he had come to Maine, he had been advised to join the Republican party because this was the only way his vote in the primaries would count; the Democrats seldom had sufficient candidates to fill out an election slate, much less enough to run against each other in primaries; his friends had told him that in the final election, of course, he could vote for either party. In the 1954 primaries, upset by the appearance of the McCarthy-oriented Jones, he naturally preferred Margaret Smith for the Republican nomination. This was still some time before he had any idea that he himself would run against her.

Fullam, who had won great respect throughout the state, had only a few more months to live. Taxed by the exhausting campaign he had waged, he suffered a heart attack and died. He is still remembered fondly by Maine Democrats as their "academic dean."

~ 11 ~

Margaret Smith, though she refuses to leave Washington while Congress is in session, declining invitations to the most important ceremonies and events if there is the slightest chance of missing a roll call, makes up for it once Congress has adjourned. It is then that she makes her regular treks across the state, renewing contacts with old friends and learning what the people like and don't like about their government; and it is then that she takes those extensive trips abroad that have played such a dominant part in her understanding of American policy.

Of all the trips she has made to various parts of the world, the one on which she set off at the end of the 1954 session of Congress, and which carried over into early 1955, was certainly the most important. As she planned it, the trip was to bring her into contact with both the leaders and the ordinary people of countries throughout Europe and Asia. The vast continent of Asia interested her particularly as the Chinese Communists began to extend their influence beyond their own borders. What contributed to making her trip extraordinary was a request from Edward R. Murrow, later the Director of the United States Information Service, but then an official of the Columbia Broadcasting System. It occurred to Murrow that moments of special interest could be re-corded for his news feature program, *See It Now,* if Margaret Smith would agree to meet CBS cameramen at different points in her journey and let them "eavesdrop" on her inter-views with local political leaders. Margaret Smith agreed, provided the foreign leaders she was to meet raised no objec-tions. She made it clear to Murrow from the beginning that her trip was primarily to gather information that would enable her to serve better in the Senate, and that the inter-views would merely be a sidelight of her trip. She received no fee or expense money from CBS.

The trip was divided into two parts, because the important censure motion against Senator McCarthy was to be pressed in December. She wouldn't miss that for the world, or a trip around it. After the censure debate, she would set off again on her travels. In early October she left New York's Idlewild Airport for London, accompanied by her assistant, William C. Lewis, and a couple of CBS cameramen.

England proved to be instructive, but not particularly rich in material for the Murrow program. The climax of her visit there was a 15-minute chat about world affairs with Eng-land's Prime Minister, Sir Winston Churchill, at his official residence at Ten Downing Street. The CBS cameramen were not invited. As she was leaving Sir Winston, who showed her to the door, Anthony Eden, later England's Prime Minister, arrived. The cameramen, waiting outside, took some good candid shots of her chatting with England's two most power-ful political leaders.

Later she prepared a transcript of her interview with Sir Winston and sent it to him for his approval, hoping to be able to give Murrow's *See It Now* audience a summary of its contents. But England was in the throes of a dock strike. Occupied with that and other problems of government,

Churchill never had the time to review the transcript, and the subject was dropped.

Though the cameramen followed her around London, and to some other English cities, there was nothing to match the importance of her talk with Churchill. Before leaving England, Margaret Smith had a five-hour interview with what had been described as a typical London family. She discussed with them employment, food, housing, children, and other subjects which concern "little people" everywhere. She was pleasantly surprised to learn that the husband was a telephone operator by night, but the sudden revelation that he was a bookie by day blighted the interview.

Then she was off to Paris. There she met Premier Pierre Mendès-France, and was confronted with one of those moments which can ruin a lady's trip. Just before being introduced to Mendès-France, she looked down at her shoes.

"I was horror-stricken," she said later. "My shoes not only didn't match what I was wearing . . . they didn't match each *other!* One was black and the other a bright navy color. My face was another color still—red!"

But Mendès-France was a model of French diplomacy. He didn't notice.

There was trouble in Madrid, but Margaret Smith was not aware of it at the time. It came about because her arrival there nearly coincided with that of another American, named Fulton Lewis, Jr. Lewis was a radio commentator distinguished by his admiration for Far Right causes at home and Far Right leaders abroad. One of his heroes was the Spanish Fascist dictator, Generalissimo Francisco Franco. Any specific criticism of Franco in America brought a charge from Lewis that the speaker was a "left-winger" or a "pinko." Visiting Spain for the first time, Lewis confidently expected an enthusiastic welcome, and a lengthy interview with his hero.

The Spanish press lived up to his fondest expectation. On the day of his arrival in Madrid the newspaper *Ya* ran a prominent and suggestive headline: TAKE OFF YOUR HAT TO FULTON LEWIS. It was accompanied by a story telling its readers that Lewis had been a true friend of the Spanish People. But Lewis' happy glow quickly faded. He learned that his request for an interview with Franco had been turned down because the dictator had already scheduled one for that week. With whom? With Margaret Chase Smith, who was interviewing Franco for Edward R. Murrow's program.

Lewis was furious. Margaret Smith and Ed Murrow were two of the most outspoken enemies of his friend, Senator McCarthy. He told his Spanish hosts exactly what he thought of such a scandal. To inquiring reporters he burst out: "It's not fair for a Senator to use her entrée for commercial purposes. Why does Murrow have to use a skirt who is a Senator?"

Spanish officials, gravely embarrassed, urged Franco to change his mind. He finally agreed to meet Lewis, but by that time the offended American broadcaster was on his way out of the country.

In East Berlin, Margaret Smith became entangled in a more serious affair. Iron Curtain countries are usually careful to present their brighter face to visiting dignitaries from the West, but Margaret Smith's visit to East Berlin was unheralded. She had stopped in West Berlin on her way to Czechoslovakia and Russia. With William Lewis (her assistant), a couple of Murrow's TV crew and United States information officer Elmer Cox, she entered the Communist sector for a brief tour. The party rode in two black State Department Pontiacs, driven by German chauffeurs.

Interested in how people shop, Margaret Smith wanted to visit a Communist department store. The party stopped at

East Berlin's biggest store, located on the busy Alexander-platz, and went in to look around. She examined a number of items on sale, asked a few questions, and returned to the sidewalk to look at the window displays. The CBS camera-men continued to take pictures of her.

At that point a burly man wearing a Soviet-German Friendship button in his lapel appeared out of a crowd of gawkers and announced that picture-taking was forbidden. The Americans ignored him. Growing nasty and officious, the stranger threatened to call the police. When he left to carry out his threat, CBS correspondent Robert Hottelet decided it would be wise to leave. He whisked Margaret Smith to one of the Pontiacs, and told the chauffeur to drive off. By this time a crowd had gathered. An East German tried to keep the Pontiac from departing by standing in front of it, but the frightened driver furiously revved the engine, and the East German leaped out of the way quickly.

Margaret Smith had narrowly escaped the unusual ex-perience of being arrested. The group in the other Pontiac, having been slower to start, was not as lucky. Lewis, Cox and a CBS sound man named Robert Huttenlock were stopped by a couple of armed, blue-uniformed "People's Police." They were hauled off to the police station, where they were held until Cox identified himself, and Lewis pro-duced his passport with the attached visa permitting him to visit Russia. That impressed the "People's Police." They released the Americans with the assurance that it had all been "a mistake."

The United States Government did not let the matter drop there. Through Major General George Honnen, the American commander in Berlin, it registered a strong protest with the Soviet commander, claiming that the incident was "a definite violation of Allied rights in Berlin." Margaret Smith, mean-while, was heading farther into the Communist world.

She arrived in Moscow just in time to witness another "incident." There was hard feeling between American and Soviet officials over the arrest there of two American women. One of the women, the wife of a secretary at the United States embassy in Moscow, had been called by the Russians "a hooligan and an undesirable." Margaret Smith herself found Moscow reasonably quiet. She was amazed at the prevalence of women in the capital, and at the lack of men in the streets.

"I asked on several occasions where the men were," she later told Josephine Ripley of *The Christian Science Monitor*, "but I never got a satisfactory answer."

All about her she saw women workers—in the factories, on collective farms, in the stores, and at a maternity hospital, where most of the doctors were women. She found the women better dressed than she had expected; in the city they had permanent waves, wore lipstick, and bought large hats ornamented with bows and feathers. She attended a fashion show in a large department store. Everywhere she went she was treated courteously, and she had an hour's interview with Soviet Foreign Minister V. M. Molotov, who told her that one quarter of the members of Russia's parliament (the Supreme Soviet) were women.

Yet the petty incidents she had seen or heard about behind the Iron Curtain emphasized for her the irreconcilable aspects of the two systems—communism and capitalism. When she arrived on free territory again, in Helsinki, Finland, she created a minor sensation by telling reporters: "I would not be surprised if the relations between the United States and the Soviet Union were broken off at any time by either side."

Her fears were not realized; President Eisenhower's meeting with Soviet leaders Nikita Khrushchev and Nikolai Bulganin at Geneva the following summer eased some of the tension between the two great powers. Meanwhile, Margaret Smith returned briefly to Washington where Senator McCarthy's career was effectively blighted by the censure motion voted against him by his colleagues in the Senate. Though he was re-elected to the Senate in 1956 during the Eisenhower sweep, he was never taken seriously again, and died before he could complete his term of office.

Margaret Smith completed her world tour early in 1955. She visited Formosa, where she interviewed General Chiang Kai-shek. In Burma she interviewed Premier U Nu, and in India she met Prime Minister Jawaharlal Nehru (and rode on a bullock). In Tokyo, speaking before a large audience of Japanese women, she said that she "wanted to hear first hand if my country has been doing anything that Japan does not want. We meet some narrow-minded people in my country but we should not criticize any country through our contact with a few." She made a big hit in Japan.

Returning to America, she announced a couple of the conclusions she had come to after traveling around the world: "The best way to fight Communism in Asia and Africa is to expose it for what it is—modern-day colonialism. I believe we have won a very definite victory in Europe. Now our principal struggle with Communism is in Asia."

The series of interviews and travel sequences shown on *See It Now* were highly successful. Presented on CBS-TV early in 1955, the interview with Chiang Kai-shek created headlines because of the Nationalist Chinese leader's assertion that he planned to invade the Chinese mainland. The programs, and Margaret Smith's part in them, were applauded by television critics. John Crosby, writing in the New York *Herald Tribune*, had this to say:

"As an interviewer the Senator has been self-effacing, letting the interviewees do all the talking and confining her role to the questions alone—and some pretty good questions."

And J. P. Shanley, writing in *The New York Times*, reported that the program was in expert hands. "Mrs. Smith not only is a gracious lady," he wrote, "she asks intelligent questions and appears at ease on camera. . . . The lady knows how to put on a show."

⪜ 12 ⪝

Now a Senate veteran, the distasteful McCarthy battles behind her, secure in the confidence of her colleagues ("No one excels her in diligence and sustained attention to duty," Senate Republican leader Everett Dirksen has said), Margaret Smith began her second term. She was still a lone woman among ninety-five men in the Senate. Whatever she chose to say, on whatever topic, was news, for time had not dimmed her attractiveness to the public.

In a speech to a group of Republican women in the spring of 1955 she created a national uproar by saying that she did not believe President Eisenhower would run for re-election the following year. His recent heart attack, she suggested, would make him reluctant to expose himself to four more years in office, and Republicans had better begin to think about a successor to him. Republican politicians, wondering how they would manage without Ike's coattails to ride into office, were inconsolable until the President reassured them he would run again. He shrugged off Margaret Smith's statement as just another example of the mysterious ways in which women work.

Like all the better legislators, she frequently proposes changes in our system of government, and like all such proposals they are beaten down by those who are eternally suspicious of change. As early as 1956 she was speaking out for changes both in our use of the old-fashioned electoral college for choosing our Presidents, and for the way we nominate candidates for the Presidency. As with so many people in government, it has been her fear that, because of the electoral college, we may someday elect a "minority President"— one most Americans did not choose but who received the most electoral votes. She advocated election by direct vote; the man who gets the most votes throughout the country thus becomes President, without all the intermediate folderol of capturing individual states. And for the process of selecting the candidates themselves, she suggested that we abandon the selection of Presidential candidates in convention, or behind the scenes in "smoke-filled" rooms. Candidates, she held, should rightfully be chosen through the direct vote of the people.

"I am admittedly prejudiced in the matter," she said in 1956. "I never could have been nominated or elected to the Senate if I had had to wait to be chosen by the party leaders." Reminding her colleagues that Senators themselves were once chosen by state legislatures, and not by the direct vote of the people, she urged them to revamp the system of selecting our Presidents. Though she received a good deal of publicity for her proposal, she got little backing in the Senate.

She was alert to defend both her constituents and the American public in matters which she believed affected them adversely. After the Suez crisis in late 1956, when the brief war there had damaged the canal and disrupted the shipment of oil from the Middle East, American oil companies quickly raised their prices. Margaret Smith's anger was as intense (if not as well publicized) as that of President Kennedy when certain steel companies unexpectedly raised their prices some years later. Aware that the homes of many struggling people in Maine were heated by oil, she sharply attacked the oil industry's opportunism.

"It is entirely possible," she said, "that prices were not raised by the American oil producers prior to the Suez crisis for the very obvious factor of foreign competition. Perhaps domestic producers didn't dare increase prices for fear they would lose such markets as New England."

She spoke out just as forcibly in the 1957 integration crisis at Little Rock, Arkansas. While many conservatives deplored President Eisenhower's use of federal troops to force Arkansas Governor Orval Faubus to obey the law, Margaret Smith took her stand with the President.

"Governor Faubus issued a challenge which the President could not ignore," she said. "Otherwise the struggle for civil rights would end in a shambles and the position of the Presidency would be reduced to impotency." Going further into the problem, she added: "The solutions will not come as the result of laws which are passed or decisions which are handed down by the Supreme Court. The really unpleasant and difficult job will of necessity have to be done by the executive, whose task it is to enforce the laws."

This comment, at the time, appeared to be a way of passing the buck; later developments in the civil rights struggle have proven Margaret Smith to be something of a prophet.

While she often spoke out against the flaws in both her party and her party leaders ("The Republican party has gotten into trouble because it has resisted change," she said in 1957), she had deep faith in the Republicans. When she had already made up her mind to vote against the controversial Dixon-Yates bill, her Republican colleagues in the Senate gave up her vote as lost; the lady seldom changed her mind. But President Eisenhower called her from Camp David and asked her to vote for the bill as a personal favor to him. She did.

But no one in either party put anything over on her. She came well prepared (as we shall see later) to ask questions in committee, and often her excellent memory provided her with other questions. When the administration had nominated veteran Congressman Dewey Short as Assistant Secretary of the Army in 1957, he appeared before the Armed Services Committee in his bid to have the appointment confirmed. There seemed to be no objections to his confirmation until Margaret Smith suddenly asked him if he had changed his opinion since 1948, when he expressed himself in vigorous terms against giving women regular status in the armed forces. Momentarily confused, Mr. Short gathered himself together sufficiently to assure the Senator from Maine that he had become reconciled to the idea. His appointment was thereupon confirmed.

All that transpires behind closed committee doors is not deadly serious. During one meeting of the Senate Armed Services Committee, Chairman Leverett Saltonstall of Massachusetts, using the rhetorical flourishes beloved by legislators, referred to Georgia's Senator Richard Russell as "the distinguished former chairman, whom we all love."

Russell, a strait-laced bachelor, seemed overwhelmed by the flattery, and Saltonstall bowed and corrected himself.

"I mean, whom we all *admire*," Saltonstall said.

"Oh, please don't change it, Mr. Chairman," Margaret Smith said coyly.

Another Senator asked if the Senator from Maine wished to go on record with her "love" for the Senator from Georgia. A good deal of teasing and laughter followed. The story, repeated outside the committee, quickly spread around Washington and before anybody realized it there was a flood of rumors pertaining to the Senate's "most eligible couple."

It isn't any wonder that the well-publicized Margaret Smith became (in those days before the Kennedys took over) a prime target of the invitations sent out by Washington hostesses. Her attendance at a party would be a major social event. Washington, like all cities crowded with exiles (and the people who work in Washington are exiles, for a good part of the year, from their home states), is a party-goer's paradise. Even in the early days of the Republic, Washington had this quality, and Senator Maclay of Pennsylvania was prompted to express his fear of the many government social functions he saw going on around him:

"From these small beginnings," Maclay wrote, "we shall follow on nor cease, until we have reached the summit of court etiquette and all the frivolities, fopperies and expense practiced in European governments."

There are politicians who have been able to adapt themselves to the swirling social life of Washington, keeping up the pace demanded by their hostesses and by their jobs. In our time, one of the men who survived, we may even say flourished, in this atmosphere was Rhode Island's Theodore Green, who, when he retired at ninety-three, was the oldest man ever to have served in the Senate. In his book, *U. S. Senators and Their World*, Donald R. Mathews tells of the struggle even Senator Green had to keep up with his social obligations in Washington. A friend spied him one evening at a party thumbing through a little black book.

"Are you trying to find out where you're due next?" the friend asked him.

"No," Green said. "I'm trying to find out where I am now."

Yet, in adjusting themselves to the social life, politicians must always be careful of their reputations. The story is told of one Midwestern Senator who had his picture taken at a wedding reception holding a glass of champagne. The next day he called his assistant and asked him to locate the negative and have it destroyed.

"If it had been a plain old glass of bourbon the folks back home wouldn't care. But champagne . . . !"

And how much more important it is for a woman, especially a single woman, in Washington to watch her every move! As Representative Frances Bolton of Ohio has said, "A woman in public office has a heavy responsibility toward all women. She must be impeccable in her habits."

There are few other Senators in history who have kept themselves as far above the dinner and cocktail circuit as Margaret Smith. She has frequently even turned down invitations to the White House, generally pleading the press of business which, to most hero-worshipers, is hardly an excuse at all. But, in her case, it is not really business either.

"I generally don't enjoy cocktail parties or big dinners," she says. "I just can't see that either the hosts or the guests really get much out of them."

Sometimes she entertains at her home in Silver Spring, Maryland (perhaps serving boiled lobster, flown to her from Down East), or at her summer place at Cundys Harbor, Maine. After her mother's death, she gave up the old house on North Avenue and moved into a rambling, white, ranch-style house which she herself designed. Furnished with mellowed mahogany and fruitwood antiques, it stands high above the Kennebec on Norridgewock Avenue, and through its broad windows one can look across the blue, log-jammed river to the tall elms and quiet farms on the far shore. She entertained President Eisenhower and his party there in 1955. Now the house stands vacant most of the year.

One outside activity she considered pertinent to her legislative duties was the period she spent as a member of the Air Force Reserve. The experience and knowledge she picked up there have, she claims, been invaluable to her in making important decisions on the Armed Services and Space Committees in the Senate. She had been appointed a Lt. Colonel in the Air Force Reserve on July 17, 1950. Afterward she devoted a good deal of her time away from Congress to fulfilling the demands of her commission; these included active tours of duty on which she visited Air Force bases or on which she worked in the Air Force's office of legislative liaison at the Pentagon. On these tours she applied herself to the study of special problems involving the Air Force.

Perhaps her most extensive tour of duty was that taken in 1957. She traveled for 30 days, visiting Air Force installations in both the United States and Germany. Her tour's most memorable experience was in becoming the first woman member of Congress to break the sound barrier. It was as a passenger on a flight made in a supersonic F-100F Super Sabre from Los Angeles' International Airport on December 10, 1957. Wearing a bright orange flight suit and high-heeled pumps, she climbed into the jet and roared off at more than 1,000 miles an hour over Southern California and the Pacific Ocean. "I felt as if I was in my living room looking out the window at the ocean and mountains," she said. "It was a wonderful experience and it was difficult to believe we were traveling at such high speed."

Upon landing again in Los Angeles, however, her hair was so disarranged by the helmet and mask she wore that she quickly called for a comb. Only then did she permit photographers to take her picture. Among those welcoming her back to solid ground was J. H. "Dutch" Kindelberger, Chairman of the Board of North American Aviation.

"Maybe some time in the future we'll invite you to take a ride in space," he told her.

Margaret Smith immediately accepted.

The purpose of her tour of duty was not to subject herself to speeds of 1,000 miles an hour, but to find out why so many missile technicians were leaving the Air Force and what could be done about persuading them to stay. After talking to many of the men and their families, she came to some interesting conclusions.

"Unhappy wives have as much to do with the men leaving as the lure of civilian salaries does," she said. "The Air Force has got to start catering to wives and do something about the lack of housing, community life, schools and recreation facilities."

In a speech at the Strategic Air Command headquarters in Omaha, she probed deeper into the problem, and offered a more complex solution.

"It seems to me," she said, "that inevitably the solution must be that such technicians are going to take on half-and-half roles, in which they are half civilian and half serviceman. Their work must be integrated between the firm they are employed by and the service, because the armed services simply cannot compete with private industry in a wage war."

Such a solution, of course, would require a strong and active reserve which, ever since her first contact with it, has been one of her most enthusiastic projects. She is deadly serious about it, and is always on the alert against those whose actions imply that they do not agree with her. This seriousness and alertness led to one of the most bizarre battles in Washington since Senator McCarthy left the scene.

❧ 13 ❧

On February 23, 1957, President Eisenhower, acting on the advice of the United States Air Force, nominated Colonel James Maitland Stewart of the Air Force Reserve for promotion to brigadier general. Stewart's name, along with the names of a number of other high-ranking reserve officers, was sent to the Senate, to be approved (as the law requires) by that body. Such promotions are generally acted on as a matter of routine, and approved without fuss or publicity.

But this was an unusual case. The Colonel Stewart in question was known to millions of movie fans as Jimmy Stewart, the star of dozens of pictures, the man who played the part of Charles A. Lindberg in *The Spirit of St. Louis* and more recently the man who played the lead role in the important Air Force picture, *Strategic Air Command*. Moreover, Jimmy Stewart was not a greenhorn who flew planes only in a Hollywood studio. Enlisting as a private in the Army Air Forces at the beginning of World War Two, he rose to the rank of colonel, flew 20 bombing missions over Germany, was named commander of a B-17 wing in the Eighth Air Force, and was decorated for heroism. Besides his status in the Air Force Reserve, Stewart flew his own Cessna 310. It seemed to the Air Force that Stewart's promotion was more than a matter of simple routine; with his credentials, it should have been approved with huzzahs.

Before a nomination for promotion to high military rank is put to a vote in the Senate it is first screened by the Armed Services Committee, and that is where Jimmy Stewart and the Air Force came a cropper. Margaret Smith, long known as a champion of the reserve forces (she has introduced a great deal of legislation in that area), had been alerted to Stewart's promotion by prominent members of the Air Force Reserve. Deserving men were being passed over, they claimed, while "celebrities" were advanced above them. Margaret Smith began an investigation. Her legislative assistant, William C. Lewis, was a colonel in the Air Force Reserve, too; he is the son of a retired Air Force brigadier general, and he has been active in reserve affairs himself for a long time. He helped Margaret Smith prepare for the committee meeting at which Stewart's promotion would be discussed. When she arrived at the Capitol, she carried under her arm a plump looseleaf notebook which contained material enough to help her ask some very searching questions about Colonel Stewart and several others on the promotion list.

To make matters easier, the Air Force had dispatched to the committee room one of its most celebrated officers—Lt. General Emmett "Rosie" O'Donnell, its Chief of Personnel. O'Donnell, a ruddy-faced, silver-haired man, had been a fine football and baseball player at West Point, had once been an assistant football coach there, and during World War Two and the Korean war had distinguished himself in combat. When he said that the eleven officers whom the Air Force (and the President) had nominated were all deserving men, there didn't seem to be much likelihood that anybody would disagree. Margaret Smith had some questions.

How was it, she wanted to know, that some of the men on the list were being promoted to very important positions when they had done little active duty since World War Two, a dozen years before?

O'Donnell said that war experience counted in promotions, and so did a man's "national reputation." He then boasted that, as Chief of Personnel, he had been very tough, booting 68,000 men out of the reserve because their training "wasn't good enough."

"In view of this severity," Margaret Smith replied, looking over the record of one of the other men on the promotion list, "why are you promoting Robert L. Smith, whose record isn't good enough either?"

She went on to say that Smith had had only one 15-day tour of duty in eight years, a violation of reserve requirements.

"General Smith was on duty December 10 to December 31, 1956," O'Donnell shot back.

Margaret Smith looked down at her looseleaf notebook. "I don't see that in the records that the Air Force sent me," she said.

O'Donnell nodded emphatically. "December 10 to December 31."

Knowing she had caught O'Donnell in a misstatement, she followed up her attack. Why, she wanted to know, was Stewart up for promotion, when 1,900 other eligible colonels had been ignored? Though he was not qualified to fly any Air Force plane then in operation and had put in only nine days of reserve training in eleven years, he was being recommended for a promotion that would place him in the position of deputy director of operations at SAC headquarters in the event the United States went to war.

"Stewart has made a great contribution to the Air Force," O'Donnell said. "We don't think we should promote people to general officer merely on the basis of a good attendance record."

Margaret Smith continued to ask questions about the names on the promotion list, contending that several of them were not qualified for promotion, and catching O'Donnell in a number of additional mistakes. At the end of the hearing she requested that the Armed Services Committee turn down several of the nominations for promotions. The committee promoted Robert L. Smith out of courtesy to his friend, Senate majority leader Lyndon Johnson, but bowed to Margaret Smith's demands in the other cases, rejecting the promotions of Stewart and J. B. Montgomery. The latter had retired from the Air Force to take a high-salaried position in private industry, and also wanted his general officer's rating restored.

Stewart took the rebuff gallantly. "I was very honored to receive the nomination by President Eisenhower and the Air Force," he said. "I intend to continue to do my best to fulfill my duty requirements as a reserve officer in the Strategic Air Command."

But a storm was brewing. The Armed Services Committee, following its normal procedure before printing the final testimony taken during the hearing, sent a transcript of that testimony to General O'Donnell to see if he had any corrections to make in it. Later, O'Donnell, with the correct information in front of him in his Pentagon office across the Potomac from the Capitol, altered 43 of the 49 pages of his testimony. Margaret Smith immediately returned it to him, asking that he confine himself to editing grammatical mistakes in the transcript and not to change the answers he had given earlier.

What happened then is still murky, but out of it grew one of the bitterest feuds Washington has witnessed in years. Rumors spread through the Capitol, and some were printed in the press, to the effect that Margaret Smith's battle against the Stewart promotion was motivated by "sour grapes." One tale had it that she was angry because William Lewis, her assistant, was one of those Air Force Reserve colonels passed over for promotion. Another, even more absurd, rumor was that her anger was personal, stemming from the fact that she herself had been passed over for promotion to full colonel in the reserve and that, although she didn't want anybody to know her real age, she had been forced to retire at the age of sixty.

Margaret Smith, at the time, did not refer to the existence of these rumors (she never referred to them specifically), but on August 24, the day after the Senate had confirmed the promotions of the nine other men on the list, she inserted in the Congressional Record a sharp attack on General O'Donnell. She said that he had defended the Air Force's choice of Stewart for what would have been literally the number-three position in the Strategic Air Command in the event of a sudden war. She accused O'Donnell of misrepresentation and "extensive false testimony" before the committee, and of "wholesale rewriting" of the transcript. O'Donnell was stunned by the fury of her attack. Later he replied that it was customary in Congressional proceedings for a witness to make corrections of the mistakes which he claimed always occur in cases where the witness has given several hours of off-the-cuff testimony.

Senator Styles Bridges of New Hampshire, a powerful Republican, went to Margaret Smith and tried to get her to go easy on General O'Donnell, but she refused. "She's the hardest woman in the world to deal with," said Bridges, who admired her. "I give up."

While Margaret Smith remained silent on the rumors which surged through the Capitol, her friends came to her defense. They pointed out that, in the case of Lewis, she couldn't have done him more harm had she really been acting out of spite because of his failure to be promoted; in view of the present attitude at the Pentagon toward her and her assistant, Colonel Lewis' prospects for rapid promotion seemed very dim indeed. And, in answer to the charges against Margaret Smith herself, her friends replied that, in the first place, she had never made any secret of her age (even correcting newspaper accounts which listed her as being younger than she was); and that in the second place she had personally introduced legislation limiting the number of full colonels in the Women's Air Force Reserve to one—the commander. Members of the Air Force Reserve Association also came to her defense, claiming that the Stewart nomination had been destructive to the morale of the reserve.

The feud simmered underground for two years. Then, in 1959, it flared into the open again when O'Donnell was nominated by President Eisenhower as Commander in Chief, Pacific Air Forces—a position which requires a four-star general. On May 19, in a letter to the Armed Services Committee chairman Senator Richard Russell, Margaret Smith brought the ugly rumors into the open.

She wrote that O'Donnell had "caused malicious and false statements against my integrity and character" to be leaked to the press, radio and television. This information had been given her, she said, by friends in the Air Force. They had also told her that unless she withdrew her opposition to the promotions of Stewart and Montgomery (which were again proposed) the Air Force "would blacken my name from coast to coast."

These were serious charges. There were doubts raised in other quarters about O'Donnell's capacity to serve in such a sensitive position. Drew Pearson, in his syndicated column, recalled O'Donnell's statement during the Korean war which suggested that the United States should have used the atomic bomb against the Red Chinese. The statement was made after American officers had been cautioned by the Pentagon about uttering irresponsible remarks on the use of the bomb.

"As a result of O'Donnell's sound-off," Pearson wrote, "he was summoned to Washington and cautioned by General Hoyt Vandenberg, Air Force Chief of Staff. 'Obviously he doesn't speak for the Air Force,' Vandenberg said.

"Since O'Donnell is now to be put in full command of the Air Force in the Pacific," Pearson continued, "where a single bombing of the Chinese mainland near Quemoy and Matsu could lead to world war, some Senators are apprehensive over O'Donnell's tendency to shoot from the hip."

It is true, of course, that O'Donnell may have been an advocate of "Gunboat Diplomacy" (an attitude which goes back to the time when a United States warship, to support American aims, had only to steam up to a fractious town and plop a couple of shells into it). But Margaret Smith could not very well hold that against him; she had rattled a few A-bombs herself.

In any case, the atmosphere in Washington was strongly reminiscent of that during 1954 when Senator McCarthy took on the United States Army in front of a national television audience. Senator Russell, acting on Margaret Smith's note (which said she had disqualified herself from the committee hearings on O'Donnell's promotion), summoned O'Donnell before the Armed Services Committee.

Now he closely questioned O'Donnell, who denied that he had done anything to blacken Margaret Smith's reputation. Secretary of the Air Force James H. Douglas was also questioned by the committee. Finally, in the absence of Margaret Smith, the committee, by a vote of 12 to 1, approved O'Donnell's promotion to four-star general. Only Harry Byrd, the Democratic Senator from Virginia, voted against it.

Shortly afterward, Jimmy Stewart's nomination again came before the committee. He had squeezed in his required flying time just before his nomination. Margaret Smith, after being assured by the Air Force that in the event of war Stewart would be given a public relations assignment, said she had no objections to his promotion. The good news was flashed to "General" Stewart, then on location for a war movie called *Mountain Road*. The cast gathered around and, to their cheers, the picture's technical adviser, retired Army Brigadier General Frank Dorn, pinned stars on the collar of the excited, grinning Stewart's film costume, which happened to be an officer's shirt.

And so the battle of "the lady Senator vs. the movie idol" came to an end. Defeated in the promotion of "Rosie" O'Donnell, Margaret Smith had made her point in the case of Stewart. Later that year, she would cast a weighty vote in another celebrated struggle over an administration appointment.

～ 14 ～

Positions of public responsibility often bring out the worst in people. Transported to Washington, they not only retain the notions and prejudices of their native area; they apply them to new situations to the point of becoming a national embarrassment. Other public servants, as Woodrow Wilson suggested, "grow" in office. Provincial or isolationist when they arrive in Washington, they find that contact with people from all over America, and from all over the world as well, impresses on them a sense of the complexities of statesmanship. Richard M. Nixon is an example of a man who grew in office. A talented but narrow politician when he arrived in Washington as a Congressman, he adjusted to the twentieth century and became one of our strongest advocates of international cooperation.

Along with this growing awareness of the United States as linked in an inextricable bond with the other nations of the world is the development of the kind of judgment which tells a legislator when he must stand his ground, and when he must compromise. John F. Kennedy, writing of his own days in the Senate, had this to say:

On the winning team in 1916, Margaret Chase (second from right), the future Senator Smith, poses with the Skowhegan (Maine) high school basketball squad which won the state championship.

Wide World Photo

Just like old times. Senator Margaret Chase Smith gets back into temporary harness during a visit to the telephone building in Atlanta, Georgia, when she was honored by a group of the city's telephone women in 1951. Senator Smith was once employed by the Maine Telephone and Telegraph Company in her home town of Skowhegan, Maine.

Campaigning in 1960 as the lone woman Senator in Washington, Republican Margaret Chase Smith greets members of the Portland (Maine) Women's Club. Mrs. Smith, at the left, wears a red rose, traditionally a part of her attire.

Wide World Photo

At a meeting of the United States Senate Armed Services Committee, Margaret Smith confers with two other committee members, Senator J. Glenn Beall of Maryland (center) and Senator Barry Goldwater of Arizona. Mrs. Smith is renowned for her diligent attention to committee work, and for her directness in examining committee witnesses.

Above: While on a world tour in 1954 to obtain firsthand information about conditions abroad, Senator Smith was greeted by Prime Minister Winston Churchill at 10 Downing Street in London.

Below: Margaret Chase Smith interviews India's Prime Minister Jawaharlal Nehru in his own office.

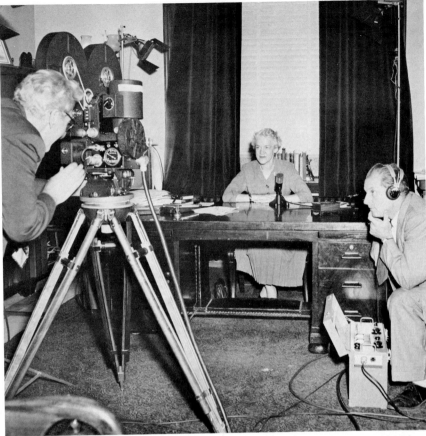

Margaret Chase Smith's world tour in 1954 marked the first exclusive report by a television program of a global journey and the first such trip guided by a United States Senator. Here, CBS technicians are shown with Senator Smith in her Washington office.

Above: As a member of the Senate Armed Services Committee, Margaret Chase Smith tours the main line of resistance at the United States naval base at Guantanamo Bay, Cuba. *Below:* With Rear Admiral Edward J. O'Donnell, Senator Smith visits the "ship's store" at Guantanamo Bay.

Senator Smith relaxes on the couch in her Capitol office during a marathon civil rights session in the Senate.

"The way to get along," I was told when I entered Congress, "is to go along." Going along means more than just good fellowship—it includes the use of compromise, the sense of things being possible. We should not be too hasty in condemning all compromise as bad morals. . . . This is no real problem, some will say. Always do what is right, regardless of whether it is popular. Ignore the pressures, the temptations, the false compromises.

That is an easy answer—but it is easy only for those who do not bear the responsibilities of public office.

Margaret Smith, like other good Senators and Congressmen, quickly became aware of those complexities which, when issues are acted upon with them in mind, may give the constituents back home the notion that their representatives have betrayed their trust. The subtleties of government may not be distinguishable to the voter back home. He usually sees from a distance only large blocks of black and white. At times, Margaret Smith's decisions in the Senate seem inexplicable to those who voted for her in Maine. But, in making her decision on the spot, she must take into consideration not only the wishes of her constituents, but the knowledge which has been made available to her, uniquely, as a Senator.

It is also true that Margaret Smith has gone in considerably less for the compromises and "deals" by which most politicians "get along." She has remained primarily a "loner" in this clubbiest of institutions. Often it might have been easier for her to give in and go along with the Senate's hierarchy, or her own party, or even the President. Yet she has insisted on making her own way. Her success in the Senate is, to a much greater extent than that of most of her colleagues, based simply on her integrity and her astounding capacity for work.

"When we have a roll call I usually go down the list one ahead and mark how I think the man's going to vote," says

Mike Monroney, Oklahoma's Democratic Senator. "I don't miss very many, but when I come to Margaret there's usually a question mark, because you seldom can figure for sure what she's going to do. But I wouldn't think of asking her. You never see anybody around her desk trying to change her, either."

And so, through the last years of the Eisenhower administration, Margaret Smith walked her independent way. While she, like most of her Republican colleagues, advocates economy in government, she will ignore these principles when she believes a certain project deserves more money. In 1958, when Eisenhower asked Congress to appropriate money for the building of four atomic submarines, Margaret Smith urged that eight of them be built. She also urged appropriations for the building of more intercontinental bombers and missiles than the President had asked for.

"Some may call this selfish of me," she said of her proposals. "But the truth is that in all good conscience I have been acting in the best interest of the nation as well as of the state of Maine."

What she was referring to was the growing concern that America's huge defense budget is based, not on national need, but on the demands of local industry that the Congressmen representing their districts bring them as many defense contracts as possible. Murray Kempton, writing in *The New Republic,* has said:

> The $50 billion defense budget has grown without effective resistance because it fattens on the demands of Congressmen for their districts and because it diverts private corporations from their pride in their independence and from that concern with fiscal stability which overcomes them when they confront a child on a relief role.

This, of course, was what Margaret Smith was referring to. The military is one of the few thriving "industries" in her lagging state. When she asked for a boost in the number of subs, bombers and missiles, she could not be abused for having had a look around her first: atomic submarines were in construction at Kittery; B-52 long-range bombers were poised at the Loring Air Force Base; and important missile bases were established in Aroostook County, all in Maine.

"Maine is just one big air base," she once said. "It is one of the most important advance fortresses within the continental limits of the United States."

But anyone who is familiar with her record is aware that she is too scrupulous and too independent to be pushed into helping her constituents at the expense of the nation at large. She will surrender her notions of fiscal stability when she believes it necessary. In 1956, for instance, when President Eisenhower asked Congress for $100 million for medical research, she recommended that $184 million be appropriated, and later she played a part in allocating $400 million for this purpose. "A country which can spend so much for tobacco and cosmetics," she said, "can afford to pay for health." And, where many Congressmen are criticized because they allow their reserve commissions in one of the branches of the armed services to make them patsies for whatever the top brass of that service requests, Margaret Smith retains the right to make up her own mind, as General O'Donnell discovered.

Many of her fiercest battles have been carried on in favor of her constituents and against the top brass. Her fury was monumental when, in 1958, she discovered that airmen at Maine's Limestone Air Force Base were being served *Idaho* potatoes. What was wrong, she demanded of Air Force Secretary James H. Douglas, with Maine potatoes? Grown in nearby Aroostook County, they would be a lot cheaper to serve than the Idahos, which had to be shipped from Idaho

Falls to Limestone, Maine. Shaken, the Air Force rectified the matter in a hurry.

A more formidable opponent than the Air Force for Margaret Smith was the combined opposition of President Eisenhower and the Navy Department in the battle over shipyard wages. Late in 1957 she proposed a bill which would bring the wages paid at the Portsmouth Naval Base (adjacent to Kittery) up to the standard paid in the Boston Navy Yard. Working tirelessly, she got the bill passed in the Senate, then used her influence to help steer it through the House of Representatives. The Navy Department, however, asked the President to veto it, which he did.

Margaret Smith's colleagues in the Senate then advised her to let the matter drop, for no Eisenhower veto had been overridden during the almost six years he had been in office; a two-thirds majority in each house of Congress is required to put a law into effect after the President has vetoed it. But Margaret Smith refused to give in. She worked night and day drumming up additional support for her bill in the Senate. And the impossible happened. On August 13, 1958, the Senate, gathered behind Margaret Smith, gave her a smashing victory, passing her bill by a vote of 69–20. A clear-cut triumph was denied her when her supporters in the House failed to muster the necessary two-thirds vote and Eisenhower's veto stood. The Navy Department, however, spurred to action by her determined drive, raised Portsmouth wages closer to the Boston standard.

On September 7, 1959, Margaret Smith received a different kind of tribute, though none the less gratifying, from her fellow Senators. Doing her job, sometimes against a background of high drama, but more often in quiet dignity, Margaret Smith had set an unprecedented record in the Senate. Not since 1955, when she had taken a day off from Washington (on the understanding, which proved to be false, that there would be no roll calls that day) to receive an honorary degree at Columbia University, had she missed a Senate roll call. Now, following a roll call vote on a farm bill, Oregon's Democratic Senator Wayne Morse began a speech on some long-forgotten topic. In the middle of his speech he was informed that Margaret Smith had just made her 700th consecutive roll call. Morse interrupted his speech to lift the rose he was wearing from his lapel and send it to her with his compliments. Immediately afterwards California's Senator Thomas Kuchel, the acting Republican leader, arose to pay her this tribute: "The people of Maine," he said, "may be proud of the record of their senior Senator."

She accepted her colleagues' congratulations without elation. "Everyone does things differently," she said. "They campaign differently. I don't judge anyone. I made a pledge when I first ran for office. I said I would stay on the job."

Margaret Smith was again a central figure in a bitter Senate battle which erupted unexpectedly during the 1959 session. It was the appointment of Lewis L. Strauss as Secretary of Commerce which touched it off. Strauss (pronounced Straws) had long been a controversial figure. A prominent Wall Street banker, he had been appointed in 1946 to the Atomic Energy Commission. From 1953 to 1958 he served as its chairman. As such he became involved in a number of public squabbles, the most significant being his action in the case of physicist J. Robert Oppenheimer. Acting as an adviser to the Atomic Energy Commission, Oppenheimer opposed the development of the hydrogen bomb and was suspended as an alleged security risk (he was later completely vindicated). Strauss' part in this case made him many enemies.

One of his bitterest antagonists was Senator Clinton P. Anderson, who had served as chairman of the Joint Congressional Committee on Atomic Energy. When, in 1959, President Eisenhower appointed Strauss Secretary of Commerce (pending Senate approval), it seemed a routine matter; only twice in the last 100 years had a Presidential Cabinet appointment been rejected. But Anderson decided to make a fight of it. He charged, before the Senate, that Strauss had through "unqualified falsehood" withheld atomic information from Congress; that he had behaved questionably in the Dixon-Yates affair; that he was vindictive toward those opposing him; and that once, after being accused of requesting security information on a scientist who opposed him, he denied the accusation only to have it proved that he had actually done so.

The Eisenhower administration threw the weight of its prestige behind Strauss' appointment. The Democrats, frustrated in their efforts to get their own legislative program approved during this session of Congress, decided to make an inter-party squabble of it, and many of its members announced they would vote against Strauss. Still Anderson could not line up enough votes to reject Strauss.

"I knew of no reason why he shouldn't be confirmed," Margaret Smith said. "But at the end of the third day of hearings I'd begun to wonder if he was the man I thought ought to head up the Commerce Department. He'd been evasive, nonresponsive, and he wasn't too careful about his facts."

Strauss, learning of her indecision, made a call on her at her office. After talking to her for half an hour, he left her with excerpts of the 1,128-page transcript of the turbulent confirmation hearings before the Interstate and Foreign Commerce Committee. Senator Anderson also left portions of the transcript with her.

There was still doubt over the outcome as the final vote approached. So bitter and extended was the debate that the roll call was not scheduled until late in the evening of Friday,

June 23, 1959. The Republicans, all of whom were believed ready to vote for Strauss with the exception of North Dakota's maverick Senator William Langer, had also won the aid of most of the Southern Democratic Senators. On the other hand, Anderson, upon finding all of the Democrats present in the Senate, with five Republicans absent, concluded that he had enough votes to win. Arkansas' Democratic Senator William Fulbright, who had decided to vote for Strauss, was persuaded by Democratic leaders to stay away. The Republicans began a frantic filibuster to delay a vote until their absent members could be rounded up. Finally, in the early hours of Friday morning, June 24, 1959, with both sides confident of victory, the roll call began.

"I'd been undecided until about eight o'clock the night before," Margaret Smith recalls. "I was still in my office and when I got up from my desk, I knew my mind was made up. Then I changed into a bright red dress—sometimes when I'm feeling a little low I put on a red dress—and went over to the Senate."

The roll call began, and went along as expected until Margaret Smith's name was called. In her quiet but firm voice she answered, "No."

There was a gasp in the ancient chamber. Arizona's Republican Senator Barry Goldwater slammed a fist against his desk, uttering an epithet gentlemen seldom used to use in the presence of ladies. The roll call then droned on to its conclusion. The Strauss confirmation was beaten by three votes, as Margaret Smith's "no" and the absence of Fulbright made the difference.

The Republican leaders were stunned, then angry. None was more angry than President Eisenhower. His purple language is reported to have far surpassed Goldwater's in both duration and variety.

"The President is more burned up about Mrs. Smith's action than about anything that has happened during his second term," one of Eisenhower's aides said. "Neither he nor the National Committee will forget the disservice she has rendered the party."

The National Federation of Young Republicans, then in session, considered "censuring" her. Stories appeared in the press which tried to explain her action. The one most frequently heard was that she was "miffed" at the White House for having ignored her many times in the past. Another suggested she was angry at the administration for not having backed her opposition to General O'Donnell's appointment. And another suggested that this was her way of getting even with Eisenhower for his veto of the Portsmouth pay raises. Margaret Smith had her own answer.

"I like integrity and I like others to be honest," she said. "I could not vote for that man."

Having ignored all the fuss about her decision, she seemed upset only at *Time* Magazine's report that Senator Anderson had told her what to do and that, upon casting her vote, she had rushed from the floor. She had, she insisted, remained there until the matter had been settled—as she always did.

There was, finally, a friendly word from one of her own party. Senate Republican leader Everett Dirksen, admitting that he was surprised and disappointed, nevertheless pointed out the Senate's long tradition of independence. "I recognize," he said, "the right of the Senate not to consent to a Presidential appointment."

Her integrity questioned, as it had sometimes been in her other unpopular votes, Margaret Smith could still fall back on her philosophy of legislation: "I work very hard on my votes and once I make a decision it's done. I don't let my votes worry me afterwards."

∾ 15 ∾

THE YEAR 1960 was especially wearing on Margaret Chase Smith, who was now sixty-two years old. In the spring she kept pace with her colleagues during the great civil rights filibuster. In the fall, after a long summer session in Washington, she returned to Maine to campaign for a third term in the Senate.

The tradition of the filibuster has evolved out of the Senate's unique nature. Because of the doctrine that in this body a small state's votes are equal to those of a big one, the Senate has tempered the rule of the majority which tends to operate in a democracy. In a sense, such restraint is beneficial, for the rights of a minority may be protected. But, because of the Senate's makeup, we often find that a situation exists which is in direct conflict with the aims of a democracy; we find the uncontested rule of the *minority!*

This queer state of affairs has occurred time and again during the long struggle over civil rights. The outnumbered Southern bloc in the Senate has stalled civil rights legislation by resorting to the filibuster—an almost interminable series of speeches which delay indefinitely the taking of a vote on a matter thought by the minority to be objectionable. Debate on an issue can be closed (in an action called "cloture") only by the agreement of two-thirds of the Senate. This is what happens, as *The New Republic* has described it:

> To apply cloture requires a two-thirds vote—67 Senators. What should be spelled out, and underlined, is that Southern votes (about 20) are not enough to win a filibuster alone. They *must* have votes of the small, privileged outside states who jealously cherish their built-in veto power. In the UN Assembly little Kuwait's vote balances off America's; but in the U. S. Senate the vote of South Dakota balances off not only New York's in a filibuster fight under the two-thirds rule, but California's as well!

The Northern liberals, fighting to pass civil rights legislation, decided to try to break the filibuster by keeping the Senate in session twenty-four hours a day. Under such pressure it was reasoned that the voices of the small group of Southern Senators would eventually falter, and then the desired legislation could be pushed through. In order to keep the Senate in session a quorum (a majority of the Senate's total membership) must be on hand to answer the frequent quorum calls. During a filibuster, members of the Senate sleep on cots set up in a large Capitol room just a few steps from the Senate Chamber itself. As the Senate's only woman member in 1960, Margaret Smith had to find sleeping quarters of her own.

She chose to camp in her office in the New Senate Office Building, a ten-minute walk from the Capitol. Like an old-timer digging in for a long Maine winter, she stocked it with the necessities of life. She had there, like other Senators, a refrigerator and a comfortable sofa. The Senate's Sergeant at Arms supplied sheets. For a blanket she used a blue and gold afghan knitted for her by Mrs. Cora Sturtevant of Farmington, Maine ("It's light, but very warm," Margaret Smith said). When the filibuster began on February 29, she brought to her office a suitcase packed with dresses, nightgowns, underclothes, shoes and toilet articles. She stuffed her small refrigerator with fruit, eggs, salad greens, a cooked ham and Poland Spring Water. She also added bread, cereals, canned soups and instant coffee. A toaster and an electric teapot completed her "kitchen."

The days were long, and so were the nights. She breakfasted in her office, usually on black coffee, toast, honey and fruit (like every other woman, she is concerned with her figure). While eating, she looked over her mail. She lunched there too (between her normal duties), and this again was a spare meal: perhaps eggs, cereal, biscuit, fruit and coffee. Dinner was heavier. Sometimes she ate in the Senate dining room, but usually she preferred to prepare her own meal: cold ham, perhaps, with soup, cottage cheese, salad, ice cream or tapioca pudding, and coffee. In any case she ate regularly, unlike many of her male colleagues who, thrown off schedule by the filibuster's demands, could be seen in the Senate dining room or a nearby cafeteria almost any hour of the day or night. Even so, Margaret Smith couldn't help envying the service provided by the Senators' wives, who made constant trips from their homes to the Capitol, bringing fresh linen, clothing and snacks.

She summed it up in one appealing little shrug. "What a woman Senator needs is a wife," she said.

It was during the long nights that she proved both her endurance and her will. Asleep on the leather sofa under her bright afghan, she would suddenly be aware of the quorum bell's penetrating clang. No time for that extra minute in bed.

"That bell is as loud as a fire alarm," she said.

She would rise, splash some cold water on her face, dress, run a comb through her hair and walk rapidly to the Capitol. Within fifteen minutes after the quorum bell had rung, she would be at her desk in the Senate Chamber. When the Senate president or president pro-tem called out her name she would be there, as she always is, to answer. As soon as the Southern filibusterer, tired and haggard, was on his feet to resume his wandering, endless speech, Margaret Smith would get up and go back to her office.

"I'm fortunate because I can go to sleep so easily," she said. "When I go to bed I go to sleep."

Once, during the filibuster, she astonished her colleagues (weary almost to the point where nothing could impress them) by wearing three different dresses during a twenty-four-hour period. Whatever the hour, sometimes two or three times a night, for as long as the filibuster lasted, Margaret Smith arrived in the Senate Chamber looking as fresh as the rose she wore on her lapel. When it was over her record of consecutive quorum and roll calls, by then over 750, was still being spun out. The struggle, for the Northern bloc, was in vain. After more than a week of filibustering, the eighteen weary Southern Senators won a victory when the liberals agreed to a considerably watered-down Civil Rights bill.

As the summer of 1960 lengthened into fall, she began to prepare for what she believed would be her toughest Senate campaign. Indeed, she told friends that she felt she might be beaten this time (a remark explained by another friend who said, "Margaret always runs scared"). But this time there was real cause for anxiety. Unopposed in the Republican primaries during the spring, where she had found opposition before, she was now confronted by a bustling, confident Democratic organization which had assembled a strong slate of candidates. It was a measure of women's political progress that here in Maine, for the first time in the history of the United States, two women would oppose each other in an election for a Senate seat.

Margaret Smith's opponent was Lucia Cormier, a former schoolteacher who had entered politics and fashioned a successful career in the state legislature. A pleasing talker, she won over many people who, for one reason or another, had grown disenchanted with Margaret Smith. Of French-Canadian descent, she went into Maine's border towns and rattled off French like a *habitant,* charming and flattering the local voters. She had a pleasing way with the "little fellow," too. Visiting a factory on a campaign tour, Miss Cormier was introduced to a worker, who sheepishly stuck out a greasy hand for her to shake.

"That's all right," she said, grabbing the hand. "I'll wipe it off on the next fellow."

Meanwhile, grumblings could be heard around the state by those who held an ear to the ground. Margaret Smith, some voters said, had gotten by on her own for so long that she had begun to think she didn't even need voters. It is usually the constituents who sit down and write letters to their representatives in Congress; but the tables were turned now as Margaret Smith began to write letters to her constituents. Some of them were scorching.

On one occasion she literally took on a whole town. Early in 1960 the citizens of Vanceboro, on the Canadian border, learned of a proposed shift in the customs station there. Such a shift would throw many of the townspeople, who worked in the railroad yards, out of work. They wrote to Margaret Smith, asking her to help them.

She answered in her typically brisk fashion that she would do everything she could to help. Then, in the next sentence, she reminded them that in 1954 the town had given Professor Fullam 107 votes for Senator, and Margaret Smith only 67 votes. Her letter was, in effect, a lesson in the facts of political life: if the townspeople wanted her help, they must be prepared to help *her.*

"It would have been better if she had not mentioned this,"

one Vanceboro resident said. "It surprised some people when they read her letters."

After hitting them between the eyes with her little moral, Margaret Smith forgot her grudge and went to work for the people of Vanceboro. Phoning the Bureau of Customs in Washington, she asked them to review the situation. It was done, and Vanceboro's 40-odd jobs were temporarily saved.

Throughout the state other citizens received similar letters from Margaret Smith, reminding them of past or present lapses in their active support of her campaigns. Several of these letters were offered as ammunition to her opponent, but Miss Cormier refused to stoop to tactics of this nature.

Meanwhile, Margaret Smith had begun her campaign. Though paying lip service to the regular Republican organization, she banked chiefly on her own friends. In every town in the state she could summon their loyalty. Where in most states a candidate for office needs the help of the regular party, in Maine the regular party needs Margaret Smith. Richard Nixon, visiting the state in his campaign for the Presidency against John F. Kennedy, acknowledged as much in a speech at Bangor.

"You've heard of people riding in on a candidate's coat-tails," he told his audience. "Here in Maine we're hanging on as hard as we can to Margaret's skirts."

Nixon, a shrewd politician, had made a correct analysis of the situation in Maine. Before he arrived there he asked her to campaign with him. She sent her regrets; she would be occupied by Senate business in Washington. Perhaps she had sensed that Nixon was doomed to defeat. It had been a shrewd prophecy when in 1958, at Falmouth, she had said that Nixon was a certainty to get the 1960 Republican Presidential nomination. She had enumerated his abilities before qualifying her admiration: "But he has not been able to move the hearts of the people." As an antidote she had suggested that he be paired with a Vice-Presidential candidate who had "a warm personality."

Those Maine people who grow excited about politics only once in every six years (or when Margaret Smith is running for office) pitched in to do their part for her re-election. Gatherings were organized, placards and campaign literature were distributed and potential voters were contacted by telephone. Maine was blanketed by the information that a race between Lucia Cormier and Margaret Smith was "like the office boy and the top executive trying for the same position."

From her office in Washington came lists of the names of each citizen in each county who had signed Margaret Smith's nomination papers (arranged alphabetically for each town), of those she had done favors for, and of those who had offered her their support. These lists were distributed to volunteers in the appropriate county, and each person on the list was contacted and cheerily reminded to vote. County leaders who got results were rewarded with a note from Margaret Smith herself, thanking them for their help. No wonder that she was reluctant to hitch herself to the less efficient and less enthusiastic state Republican organization. Republican leaders were happy if they could occasionally lure her into making an appearance with the rest of their slate of candidates.

Lucia Cormier was conducting a vigorous campaign of her own. Going into towns and cities all over the state, she won many friends for the Democratic party. While visiting the coastal town of Bath, she ran into a rumor for which she could not account. Was it true, people asked her time and again, that Jimmy Stewart was financing her campaign? She was asked the question so many times that she finally found it necessary to raise it during the course of her speech at a party dinner there.

"I can assure you," she told her audience, "that Jimmy Stewart is *not* backing my campaign in any manner."

Maine, having shifted its Election Day to coincide with that of the other forty-nine states, was the scene of some excitement as the race between these two determined women moved into its final stages. But, though it was a Kennedy year in most of the Northeast, Maine went Republican. Margaret Smith, in another powerful demonstration, polled 255,478 votes, 96,000 more than Lucia Cormier, for the highest total in the state's history. She ran 15,000 votes ahead of Nixon's total for the Presidency.

Among those amazed at the margin of her victory was New York's Republican governor, Nelson Rockefeller. After noting that her 61.6 percent of the state's total vote was the highest percentage won by any Republican Senator who campaigned that year, Rockefeller conferred with her in Washington.

"I wanted to see how she did it," he told reporters later.

Margaret Smith's reputation as a vote-getter was approaching her reputation as a legislator.

~ 16 ~

As 1961 BEGAN, Margaret Smith entered a new era in Washington. For one thing, she was no longer the only woman in the Senate. And for another, she was no longer a member of the party which controlled the White House; the Republicans were out, and a confident and ambitious young Democrat was the new President of the United States.

Senator Maurine Neuberger was another woman who had followed her husband into politics. She had married Richard L. Neuberger, who became a State Senator in Oregon. It had often occurred to her that wives sometimes go into partnership with their husbands in business, medicine or law. Why not politics? In 1950 she decided to run for the state legislature.

"We were both Democrats, running in a normally Republican area," Richard Neuberger once recalled. "It was like being caribou in timber wolf country."

Intelligent and skillful, the Neubergers survived as Democrats. Maurine Neuberger was elected to the state legislature, where she and her husband formed an effective team in pushing through desirable legislation. He was elected to the United States Senate in 1954, where he became an able and popular politician. After his untimely death in 1960, Maurine Neuberger made up her mind to run for his seat. And, in the fall of 1960, at the same time that Margaret Smith was defeating Lucia Cormier, Maurine Neuberger was being elected to the Senate by the people of Oregon.

On January 3, 1961, each of the Senators beginning their six-year term, both those who were coming to the Senate for the first time and those who had been there for many years, were sworn in. It is the custom at these ceremonies for each Senator taking the oath of office to be escorted down the aisle by the other Senator from his state. When it was time for Maurine Neuberger to take her oath, she was escorted forward by Oregon's senior Senator, Wayne Morse. But when Margaret Smith rose to go down the aisle she waited for Maurine Neuberger to take her arm.

Once again Margaret Smith had broken tradition, and all of Washington talked about it. She explained that she wanted Maurine Neuberger to escort her because "it was a historic occasion." Others offered a more interesting explanation: Margaret Smith had broken tradition as a rebuke to Maine's junior Senator Edmund Muskie, who had vigorously supported Lucia Cormier during the 1960 campaign.

A little over two weeks later, on January 20, John F. Kennedy was sworn in as the 35th President of the United States. It was a blustery day, and Margaret Smith was handsome in her heavy mouton fur and matching hat. It must have been with mingled feelings that she watched the inauguration ceremonies taking place on the large platform specially constructed for the occasion over the steps of the Capitol's East Front. Though a Democrat, it was a New England man who stood before Chief Justice Earl Warren of the United States Supreme Court, taking his oath of office. And, prominent too on the stand, was another New Englander, the white-haired yet vigorously alert Robert Frost, there to recite one of his poems.

Margaret Smith, unobtrusively, was taking a new position in Congress. Though her independence (and her sex) had kept her from becoming a member of the Senate's "Establishment," she had at last won not only her colleagues' admiration but a certain popularity as well. It was not that she had let down any of her barriers of reserve, or her determination to stay out of Washington's social whirl. This change could best be seen in the Senate itself. It was apparent in comments like one made by New Hampshire's Republican Senator Norris Cotton, whose seat on the Senate floor was next to Margaret Smith's. While remarking that it was indeed a "privilege and pleasure," he admitted his proximity to her had some drawbacks.

"If I leave my seat, even for a few moments," he said, "when I return I always find it occupied by some other Senator."

Margaret Smith was becoming a magnet in the sense that outstanding national politicians are magnets—drawing to them people of high estate and low who are eager to talk with them, ask them favors, and sound them out on important matters. Confronted by the power and prestige of the Kennedys in Washington, Margaret Smith was now stepping out as a leading spokesman for the opposition.

She warmed to her new task slowly. There were, for a while, the usual routine battles. Pursuing her relentless attack on the appointment of unqualified men to high positions in the armed forces, she ruffled some feathers in the new administration as she had in the old. She sharply questioned Defense Secretary Robert S. McNamara about the Pentagon's carelessness in approving the promotions of "political generals"—those men appointed to positions of command in the National Guard of the various states who, while chiefly serving as aides to the governor of their state, eventually gained status in the federal armed forces too.

"If you want to keep the military out of politics," she told McNamara, "you should be consistent and keep politics out of the military."

Secretary McNamara promised that the Pentagon would be more careful in the future.

Always sensitive to the charge that the Republican party is opposed to change (she, too, has sometimes leveled the charge), Margaret Smith continued to formulate proposals for changes in the American government. She renewed her call for a constitutional amendment which would provide for the nomination of Presidential and Vice-Presidential candidates by direct primaries early in August. "A candidate," she explained, "would qualify to enter the primary by filing a petition which had been signed by at least one percent of the total vote cast in the last Presidential election."

She insisted that this would take the selection of Presidential candidates out of the hands of party bosses and give it to the people. "And the position of Vice-President has become so important," she said, "that it should not be relegated to the status of a consolation prize, nor should it be decided by the vote of one person, the Presidential nominee, to the exclusion of the votes of tens of millions of other Americans."

She also came out for split sessions of Congress, in which the first would be held from January to August, the second from November to January. In even-numbered years the second part of the annual session would be held 15 days later because of the November elections.

"Year after year we see sessions going late into August, September or October," she said. "And we see tempers frayed, mental fatigue and exhaustion. We legislate then under conditions that are not conducive to clear minds and stable emotions."

She pointed out that under the present grueling Congressional schedule many families are separated for as much as six months of the year.

"With school recessing in June," she said, "many of the wives and children go back home while the members must remain here in Washington. Then when the mothers and children return to Washington in September for the start of school the chances are that the members have left Washington to go back home to their constituency—not to return to Washington until January."

There was a petty squabble. When Jimmy Stewart published his memoirs in the *Saturday Evening Post* early in 1961, Margaret Smith fired a blast at the Pentagon, which had called Stewart to active duty that week. Advertisements urged readers to buy the *Post* and find out "why Margaret Chase Smith opposed his nomination." She fumed at what she believed to be the Pentagon's participation in a promotion scheme to sell copies of the magazine. Stewart, in the middle once more, pleaded ignorance of any plot to embarrass his former nemesis. "I swear I didn't write an unkind word about Senator Smith."

And there was a battle in a rarer atmosphere, which finally came to include the two most powerful men in the world—and the wife of one of them. On September 21, 1961, Margaret Smith made one of her rare speeches on the Senate floor. It was, *The Christian Science Monitor* said, "one of the most memorable speeches of this year's session of Congress"; *Time* called it "a criticism, all the more scathing for its unpartisan sincerity, of the Kennedy Administration's cold war policies." It was, too, the first shot in Margaret Smith's enduring attack on the Democratic President and his administration.

She announced that she was speaking "not only to the members of the Senate but to all Americans—and most specifically to the President of the United States."

Drawing on the knowledge she had accumulated as a member of the Armed Services Committee, she said that the United States had a decided nuclear capability advantage over the Russians. "But," she added, "we are in danger of frightening ourselves—of being mesmerized by Khrushchev's confidence and deterring ourselves instead of deterring the Soviets."

She said that President Kennedy had used strong words in the crises over the Cuban invasion fiasco and Laos, but had not backed up those strong words with action. Khrushchev, she reasoned, was not afraid of our nuclear strength because he believes we won't use it.

"He sees us turning to emphasis on conventional weapons—and ironically, he has an obviously great superiority in conventional weapons and manpower over us. We have in effect played into his hands—for the kind of warfare in which he knows he can beat us. We have restricted ourselves on the freedom of choice to use the nuclear tactical weapons which he knows would defeat him if he started war.

"We have the nuclear capability, and he knows and fears it. But we have practically told him we do not have the will to use that one power with which we can stop him. We have the nuclear capability—but not the nuclear credibility."

She asked President Kennedy to stand up to Khrushchev and make him believe in our will to defend ourselves. "The greatness of this country," she said, "was not won by people who were afraid of risks."

President Kennedy was not pleased with this speech by a former Senate colleague. He told a reporter from *Look* that Margaret Smith was "ignorant." But the ripples from her speech had fanned out far beyond the White House. They had reached all the way to Moscow, for presently Margaret Smith was the target of a bitter statement by Mr. Khrushchev himself.

"Who can remain calm and indifferent to such provocative statements," the Soviet premier thundered, "made in the United States Senate by this woman, blinded by savage hatred toward the community of Socialist countries?

"It is hard to believe how a woman, if she is not the devil in disguise of a woman, can make such a malicious, man-hating call.

"I don't know whether she has children and how many, but she should understand that in the fire of nuclear war millions of people would perish, including her own children, if she has any. Even the wildest of animals, a tigress even, worries about her cubs, licks and pities them. But Margaret Smith in her hatred of everything new and progressive has decided to beat all records of savagery."

Margaret Smith accepted placidly these thunderbolts from the summit. "Mr. Khrushchev isn't really mad at me," she told reporters. "I am not that important. He is angry because American officials have grown more firm since my speech."

She had not heard the last of it from the Khrushchev family. The Soviet Premier's wife, Nina, speaking in Moscow, called Margaret Smith a "warmonger." At any rate, the Khrushchevs were far enough away from the United States Senate to feel comparatively safe from Margaret Smith's caustic remarks. President Kennedy was not quite so fortunate.

The Kennedy administration, whose bustle and confidence cloaked much of its indecision during its early days, was a plump target for the Senator from Maine. She chided not only the Democrats, but the Republicans too for the awe in which they seemed to stand of the glamorous young President. She accused prominent members of her party of "faintheartedness" because of their reluctance to step forward as possible opponents for Kennedy in the 1964 Presidential election.

"The impression, whether it be right or wrong, fair or unfair, is that they have refused to be the 1964 nominee because they don't think Kennedy can be beaten and they believe that the Republicans can't win."

But there was nothing fainthearted about her own attack on the President. Even her strongest critics among the Republicans' Old Guard were delighted by her speech before 2,000 Republican women who had gathered in Washington for a convention early in the spring of 1962. Her blue eyes sparkling, Margaret Smith entertained the women with a speech which she called "The Kennedy Twist." Recalling Kennedy's campaign promises before his election, she went on to point out over 20 occasions on which he had reversed himself (or, in her words, "did the twist") on those promises.

Recalling Kennedy's denouncement of personal diplomacy, she recalled how he had gone to Vienna shortly after taking office and had been handed by Khrushchev himself a tough ultimatum on Berlin; this Vienna "summit" meeting she referred to as "the Kennedy twist in waltz time." Describing Kennedy's reversal of his earlier stand on the B-70 bomber program, she referred to it as "the Kennedy twist in Reverse Action." And describing Kennedy's handling of the Cuban invasion and its aftermath, she called it "the Kennedy twist, done in agony with a Cuban beat."

The Republicans, discouraged till then by Kennedy's popularity across the country, ate up this rather heavy-handed humor. Her speech was reprinted by the Republican National Committee in digest form and distributed all over the country. The party asked her frequently to make speeches, helping to shore up wobbly local candidates seeking re-election.

GOP Chairman William Miller said of her: "You can put it this way. We consider her a very popular commodity."

During the squabble between the President and Big Steel over the rise in steel prices, Margaret Smith put a plague on both their houses. After having applauded Kennedy's stand against the steel owners' decision to raise their prices, she abruptly returned to the attack. "But I do not applaud the other tactics such as the threatening of criminal prosecution and the use of police state methods such as the FBI routing a reporter out of bed in the middle of night."

Perhaps the Presidential oversight which embarrassed her during the President's visit to Maine was less careless than Freudian. In the summer of 1962, when she learned that President Kennedy planned a boat cruise Down East, she sent him an invitation to visit her at her summer home on Cundys Point. She got no reply to her invitation. Finally, on the day before Kennedy's scheduled departure from Washington, she received a note from a Presidential aide (Kenneth O'Donnell) saying that the President sent his regrets, but he would not be in the area of her home. Although Senator Muskie had been invited to fly with the President to the Naval Air Station to see him off at Brunswick, Maine, there was no mention of Margaret Smith; nor was she invited to be at the airport to greet him as other Maine dignitaries were.

Undaunted, she went anyway. She flew from Washington to Brunswick in a Navy plane, and was on hand when the President arrived. Apparently the President was tipped off that somebody had goofed. He extended a cordial invitation to her to fly with him *back* to Washington, but she declined. Even Presidents cannot escape the fury of a woman scorned.

As people began to talk about the 1964 Presidential campaign, still more than a year away, there already were signs of another Vice-Presidential boom for Margaret Smith. If courage and experience counted, her admirers asked, why was she not as well qualified as anyone else to run on the Republican national ticket? Those who accepted her as a Vice-Presidential possibility were aware that they must also accept her as a Presidential possibility; the well-worn phrase that only a heartbeat divides the two positions became again a terrible reality with John F. Kennedy's assassination. Margaret Smith did not encourage her admirers. Yet, just as a candidate's religion has ceased to be a barrier to our highest office, it may yet become a mark of our political maturity that a candidate's sex has nothing to do with the matter, either.

◆ 17 ◆

"POLITICS is the people's business, the most important American business there is." The words are those of a Democrat, Adlai Stevenson, but they sum up Margaret Chase Smith's attitude toward her profession. She is in the business of running the most complicated government on earth, and its demands are infinitely diverse. Well into her sixties now, Margaret Smith met the challenge of the increasing work load her unique business had imposed on her, and filled in the rest of her day with duties she imposed upon herself.

One of the pleasures of any business is supposed to be the opportunity for travel. Yet travel for Margaret Smith is mostly hard work; its joys are usually limited to the satisfaction she gets from new experiences and the use she can put them to when she returns to Washington. As a member of the Senate Armed Services Committee, she continues to make frequent inspection trips to United States military installations. An inspection trip in which she participates is not a frivolous affair. She is no "mere woman" among a group of military men, but a presence to be deferred to, a presence which is *felt*. Always well prepared for her trips, she is able to ask pertinent (and sometimes impertinent) questions which will enable her to formulate legislation later on in the Senate.

Her inspection tour may be a routine matter, like a brief visit to a nearby naval air station (she professes a liking for Navy "chow"). Or it may be a tour as extensive and vital as the one she made to the Guantanamo Naval Base shortly after the 1962 Cuban crisis. There, within sight of Communist Cuban territory, she told American sailors and marines that their government would not negotiate with Russia or Cuba about surrendering the base.

"We cannot tolerate such a thought," she told the men. "We cannot undermine what you are doing to hold this vital base."

Earlier in 1962 she had made a trip through South America (the first extensive trip abroad she had ever made at the taxpayers' expense since coming into the Senate). Where many Congressmen and Representatives have in the past looked on these "junkets" as joyrides, Margaret Smith paid attention to what she saw and heard, and when she returned to Washington the conclusions she brought back with her were far different from the ordinary pleasantries our politicians usually exude.

"What we found in South America was not encouraging," she said. "What we found was disturbing. What we found was ingrained cynicism and a growing lack of respect for the United States. We found real and deep trouble, which the Alliance for Progress alone cannot solve and cannot stem.

"The chances are that we waited too long—for South Americans are inclined to view our efforts now as a desperate attempt to get them to save us from the threat of Castroism."

Yet, at a time when many other members of Congress favored cutting military aid to South America, she asked that we send even more military aid to these countries. "The greatest friends that the United States has in Latin America," she insisted, "are the members of the military forces. And the greatest enemies of Communism are the military forces."

Just as important to her job is the annual fall trip she makes through the state of Maine.

"Some politicians campaign only in the year they are going up for re-election," a friend of hers has said. "But Margaret campaigns *every* year . . . and she works as hard at it when the election is still five years off as she does when it's right around the corner."

If the Senate is not in session during the fall, Margaret Smith plans a two-month tour of the state. In 1959, for instance, she drove her Ford 7,158 miles through Maine, covering a territory marked off by Van Buren in the north to Kennebunk in the south, from Calais in the east to Fryeburg in the west. She made 84 talks to clubs, schools, and any other group of people which would gather to hear her. Unlike most politicians, she doesn't pass out much campaign literature. "Once you've met Margaret Smith you remember her," is the way one Maine clubwoman puts it.

She is, of course, tremendously popular. One politician (a male Republican) who shared a speaking platform with her came away shaking his head.

"After we spoke there was a reception organized so that the club members could meet the speakers. I stood next to Margaret in the reception line. Women would come up to her and hold her hand in their two hands and just look into her eyes with open admiration. Then they'd give my hand a quick little shake and move on."

As election day draws near, there is little noticeable change in Margaret Smith's activity, but her campaign takes on a more formal structure. "Success in any political campaign," she says, "demands intensely hard work, honesty and courage." It is then that the loyalty she has inspired in so many Maine people begins to pay off. Hundreds of her supporters throughout the state would never dream of working for any-body else's election. They are Margaret Chase Smith sup-porters first, and Republicans second. Others are regular party workers who like to stay on the good side of their senior Senator.

All of her campaign workers, in towns and cities alike, get plenty of help from Margaret Smith and William Lewis, her administrative assistant, who select her campaign chairmen in each country. These chosen leaders then go about lining up leaders in each town who in turn go to work on their fellow citizens. Many of these devoted workers were first charmed by Margaret Smith when they heard her speak to some small gathering in their town. They offered their sup-port, which was gladly accepted, and now they toil diligently in her cause.

"Margaret always runs scared," one campaign leader has said. And that's the way her workers pitch in and help: as if their lives depended on the election's outcome. They have to be hard workers to keep up with her. A Maine Republican who followed her around the state on one of her campaign tours reports that she was indefatigable. She arose at four o'clock in the morning, and often worked straight through until midnight.

But it is exhausting work. Margaret Smith must keep a pleasant smile on her face, be agreeable to the thousands of people she meets and prepared to make a speech at every stop. Serious about her job, she dislikes the "gimmick" photos which publicity men like to take of politicians: pictures show-ing her with a skillet in her hand, or kissing a baby, or wearing an Indian headdress. These she resolutely avoids. At the same time she must be prepared to answer the innumerable and varied questions which her audiences put to her at the end of her talks. Criticized by a member of the audience for some specific stand she has taken, she is quick to defend herself.

"I'm glad you don't agree with me on every action I take in the Senate," she will tell her critics. "If you did, then I wouldn't necessarily be representing the viewpoints of all the other people of Maine."

Despite the frequency of her trips back to Maine (she returns there at least once a month even while Congress is in session) there are people who criticize her for not returning more often. Perhaps the comments come from those who had hoped to have her speak before *their* group, and she wasn't able to fit it in. Nevertheless, you will hear people say:

"She ought to be up here lighting some fires, but she isn't. She's down there in Washington, trying to keep her voting record going."

Because conscientious Senators must spend so much time in Washington they leave themselves open to remarks like this, and are vulnerable to enemies who can spend all of their time in the home state. It is frequently the custom of dictators, when they leave their country for conferences or inspection tours, to take with them their chiefs of staff or anyone else who might attempt to seize power while they are away. But Senators must leave their rivals behind when they go to Washington, and those rivals can cause trouble.

It is in Washington, however, that Margaret Smith makes the record on which she can stand when election time comes around. There she puts in the kind of day which would wilt strong men in this age of the forty-hour-or-less week. She is up before seven at her home in Silver Spring, Maryland. After brief exercises, she dresses and prepares a spartan breakfast of grapefruit, black coffee, toast and honey, which she eats while looking out the window at the birds ("you can learn a lot from birds"). Then she leaves for the 12-mile drive to her office in Washington.

If it is to be an especially busy day, Margaret Smith may wait until she arrives in the New Senate Office Building to have breakfast; then she will send to the cafeteria for her grapefruit, toast and coffee while reading the newspapers or getting down to work.

She is keenly sensitive to the faintest shade of criticism in the Maine newspapers. If she detects what she believes is an unfair remark about her, she will dash off a letter to the culprit, if his by-line is on the story, or to the editor if it is not. A number of Maine reporters have kept as souvenirs blistering notes from Senator Smith; some display them as soldiers display their war wounds, like badges of honor.

On March 29, 1963, the Portland *Press* struck back at her. In an editorial, the *Press* wrote that Margaret Smith had changed from the earlier days of her political career when "she acquired a reputation as a non-conformist stateswoman of courage and ability and great personal charm. But lately Senator Smith has changed, until now she has become super-sensitive to honest errors, unintentional slights and objective criticism."

She reads with particular wariness the columns of May Craig, the veteran Washington columnist for Maine's Gannett newspapers. Once she and Mrs. Craig were friends. Then there was a sudden cooling between them.

"May wrote some things that Margaret didn't like," one Maine newspaperman says. "Not that it was intentional. But you have to be very careful how you phrase anything when you are writing about Margaret. And I don't think May liked it when Margaret was writing that syndicated newspaper column. She thought Margaret should stick to politics because there was room for only *one* famous woman columnist in Maine."

In any case, Margaret Smith denounced Mrs. Craig on the floor of the Senate for writing "false" stories about her. Mrs. Craig refused to strike back ("I will give only my name, rank

and serial number," she joked to reporters who asked her for
a statement) but the Portland *Press* backed her with another
strong editorial.

If Margaret Smith's breakfast has not been spoiled by what
she reads about herself in the morning papers, she throws
herself immediately into her work. She is aided by a competent staff of about a dozen people headed by Lewis and
her brother-in-law (her sister Laura's husband), Joseph A.
Bernier. The other positions on the staff are filled by women
and girls, and it is considered an honor in Maine for a girl
to be chosen to work in Senator Smith's Washington office.
A report released in 1959, for instance, showed that Margaret
Smith was paying her staff a total of about $70,000 a year in
salaries, ranging from the $16,300 paid to Lewis down to
$3,162.80 paid to four of the secretaries. Like every Senator,
Margaret Smith receives a yearly allowance from the government with which she pays these salaries. Her own salary is
$22,500 a year.

Lewis, fifty years old in 1963, has been her administrative
assistant since she was elected to the Senate in 1948. The
son of an Air Force Reserve general, he was counsel for the
House Naval Affairs Committee when Margaret Smith first
met him and admired his work. She still depends heavily on
him for advice and preparation in her various duties, though
of course she makes all final decisions herself. Lewis (who,
as a brigadier general in the Air Force Reserve, outranks
Lt. Colonel Margaret Smith) accepts the situation gracefully.
He says he handles it exactly as General James H. Doolittle
did when he was riding with a WAC aide during World War
Two. When the car stopped, the WAC looked at Doolittle
in puzzlement.

"General," she said, "you outrank me, but I'm a woman.
Who gets out of the car first?"

"Ma'am," the general answered, "beauty always precedes rank."

There is the mail to answer—sometimes two hundred letters a day. "Her office is a service agency for her constituents," a Maine politician has said. "They know that if a pension check doesn't come through they can get in touch with her and she'll do something about it."

Legislators get some strange mail, part of it flattering, part of it of the nature of the letter Arizona's Representative Morris K. Udall got not long ago. It said, in part:

"Of all the rats and snakes elected to office in Washington to represent the people and carry out their wishes, you rank head and shoulders beneath the lowest!"

The letters may contain requests for favors, or criticism of some recent vote she cast on the Senate floor, or perhaps thanks for some move she has made for the people of Maine. After she attacked the government's restrictions on oil imports (which allowed United States oil producers to raise the price of heating oil, vital to a cold state like Maine, without the hindrance of foreign competition) she received this letter from a Tenants Harbor housewife:

We like the way you look out for the interest of us ordinary folks back in Maine—whether because of letters like this or because of extraordinary awareness of the great difference between the seemingly privileged life of the average congressman with his martinis and jowls and the average state-of-Mainer trying to figure out how to pay both the dentist and the oil dealer and still have something left over for rolled oats and a bag of flour.... Maybe the Administration can see its way clear to accommodate some of us non-millionaires.

As we see it we have two choices: to switch back to the old wood-burning furnace or to write Margaret Chase Smith and hope!

Sometimes Margaret Smith receives even more flattering letters: optimistic bachelors write to ask her to marry them!

She often types out on the Smith-Corona typewriter on her desk the replies to her mail. As a Senator, she has the franking privilege: a replica of her signature which, when printed on the envelope in place of a postage stamp, enables her to send her business mail free. Like her scrupulousness about answering every roll call is her scrupulousness about answering every letter the same day it arrives. She may not have all the facts ready for a complete answer, but she sends at least a note saying the letter has been received.

Government agencies listen when a call comes through from Maine's senior Senator. A complaint from a constituent sends her into action, and a few phone calls generally set the matter straight. No bureaucrat likes to argue back when Margaret Smith makes a request. Her constituents generally are grateful for the help too. In 1959 the Maine members of the National Postal Workers Transport Association praised her for her persistent efforts to improve postal service in the state despite a cut in railroad service there. Her efforts can be very personal too. In 1962 she introduced a bill in the Senate permitting an East Eddington man, an Army sergeant, to adopt a Korean orphan.

Visitors from Maine frequently drop into the office, either to say hello or ask a favor, while they are in Washington. She always seems happy to see them.

"I do as little talking as possible when I meet my constituents," she says, "because I want to listen more to what people are saying. Then I understand what they are thinking about and how they feel about vital issues."

As the morning progresses, her work becomes more hectic. Often she sends one of her staff out to do her shopping; a tube of toothpaste or some lipstick may be all she needs, but in the press of business she hasn't had time to buy them.

Before ten o'clock she tries to complete her study of committee reports; one of the committees on which she serves (Armed Services Committee, Appropriations Committee, and Aeronautical and Space Sciences Committee) may be meeting that morning, and she wants to be prepared to question witnesses or pass on bills.

"I am not a rubber stamp Senator," she says. "I will not surrender my responsibilities."

Each committee presents its own problems. "The greatest problem of the Armed Services Committee," she has said, "is dealing with the conflicts and controversies between the Army, Navy and Air Force."

She mentioned the Air Force generals who are reluctant to face the fact that bombers are being replaced by missiles, the admirals who are reluctant to admit that aircraft carriers are being replaced by atomic submarines, and the Army generals who will not admit that the numbers of foot soldiers needed today must be reduced.

"I am convinced that we must have one service instead of the three or four who bicker among themselves as we have now. These officers are fighting a losing battle. If they don't accept the facts, the Senate Appropriations Committee will force the change."

At noon Margaret Smith leaves her office and goes to the Capitol; she prefers the ten-minute walk there, though in bad weather or in cases of emergency there is a "subway" connecting the two buildings, and a station wagon which carries those who prefer to travel above ground. In 1962 she and Senator Maurine Neuberger were each given a two-room suite in the front of the Capitol itself, with easy access to the Senate floor. Separated by a powder room, the suites look out over the plaza and serve as a place of retreat, where the lady Senators can rest during a long day of Senate business. They serve too as a substitute office for catching up on paper work. Margaret Smith has done the walls of her room like those of her Skowhegan home, in blue spruce paneling trimmed in white and decorated with gilded sconces.

When the stars and stripes go up over the north wing of the Capitol at noon, signifying that the Senate is in session (a similar flag goes up over the south wing when the House of Representatives is in session; the flag beneath the Capitol's dome remains the only one in the country which is never furled, day or night), Margaret Smith is ready for Senate business. The day's session in the grand Senate Chamber is called to order by the Vice-President, or, in his absence, by the Senate President Pro-Tem. It is opened with the Chaplain's Prayer.

A visitor from Maine who hopes to see Senator Smith on the floor may be disappointed if he arrives at the wrong time. During the long speeches which drone on during much of the time the Senate is in session she may slip away to catch up on her work or to attend a committee meeting, leaving only a handful of Senators on the floor. But if the bell rings for a roll call, she will be there. On June 15, 1961, the Senate passed a resolution commending her for "her devotion to duty" as she answered her one thousandth consecutive roll call. When the ceremony was over, Vermont's Senator George Aiken came over to her and shook her hand.

"Now, Margaret," he said, "I hope you'll go out on a bat and miss twenty votes in a row."

Apparently she didn't take his advice. As the 1963 session of Congress drew toward a close she had answered 1,400 consecutive roll calls.

She lunches, nearly always, downstairs in the Senate dining room. If she has visitors from Maine she may ask them to eat with her. Otherwise she will sit down at a table with several of her Senate colleagues for a light lunch.

While Margaret Smith does not make it a point to be conspicuous on the Senate floor (reporters in the gallery have complained that she speaks in such a soft voice that they often fail to catch her vote) she seems to stay in the thick of things. She never lets up. There or in committee she complains of government's encroachment on business, and of any sign she detects that the government's preparedness for defense has slackened. Her opposition to the 1963 Limited Test Ban Treaty was a reaction to her fear that our security was in jeopardy.

She is not above acting "inconsistently" if she believes it to be in her state's best interests. While she has battled the government's policy of protecting the domestic oil producers against foreign competition in order to keep oil prices down in Maine, she has more recently fought free trade policies because cheap foreign labor imports have hurt Maine's textile and shoe industries.

"I try to cast my vote in the way I think I would want my own representative in Congress to vote, if I were not a Senator," she says.

This accounts for the many times she votes against her own party on important issues. She has never changed in that respect, confounding her Republican colleagues as much today as she used to do back in the early 1940's when she backed Franklin D. Roosevelt on so many issues. In 1962 President Kennedy nominated John McCone to be the new director of the Central Intelligence Agency. Most of the Democrats backed the President's choice, of course, and, since McCone was known as a conservative Republican, most Republicans backed him too. There were only a few dissenters. Margaret Smith had many serious reservations. McCone, then the second largest stockholder in Standard Oil of California, would be critically entangled as CIA director in the affairs of the oil-rich Middle East. Could he be depended upon to act impartially there? Along with several

Democratic Senators, she was disturbed by the "conflict of interest" implications.

Perhaps even more important, Margaret Smith wondered about McCone's qualifications to be chief of the United States' intelligence network. She questioned him about it closely.

Sen. Smith: It is my recollection, Mr. McCone, that all of your predecessors had some prior training or experience in the field of intelligence prior to their appointment as Director of the Central Intelligence Agency. Will you tell the committee what training or experience you had in the field of intelligence prior to your appointment to that position?

Mr. McCone: None.

Sen. Smith: In view of your lack of training and experience in the field of intelligence, you are unique, are you not, in comparison with all of your predecessors?

Mr. McCone: I do not know that, because I do not know the experience of my predecessors.

Sen. Smith: What then makes you feel that you are suitably and adequately qualified to be the Director of the Central Intelligence Agency when you have had no experience or training in the field of intelligence?

Mr. McCone: I think, Senator, that that was a question decided by others than I. . . .

Sen. Smith: Was there not some question in your mind about your qualifications?

Mr. McCone: A very serious one.

Sen. Smith: Did you not raise such a question with the President and others with whom you talked?

Mr. McCone: I raised it in my own conscience, naturally. And with my wife. Yes.

Sen. Smith: But not with the President?
Mr. McCone: No; I did not raise it with the President.

Margaret Smith was one of two Republicans who voted against the confirmation of McCone as CIA director. He was confirmed anyway, but she was again in the Republican "doghouse."

Not all of her battles are on issues of national importance. Big or little, she fights with determination. One of the facts of Senatorial life is the rivalry which springs up between the two Senators from one state, especially when they are from different parties.

"The relations between two Senators from the same state are almost always strained," writes Donald R. Mathews in *U. S. Senators and Their World,* "and their competition for publicity in the same area seems to be one reason for this coolness."

Relations between Maine's two Senators were strained to the breaking point in 1960, when the junior Senator, Democrat Edmund S. Muskie, campaigned for the senior Senator's foe, Lucia Cormier. They worsened in 1961 when Margaret Smith attacked Muskie on the Senate floor. The crux of the matter was the appointment of a postmaster in Rumford, Maine. The Senate Post Office Committee does not take action on any appointment until the candidate for a position is approved by both of his state's Senators. Margaret Smith charged that Muskie had held up for two years the confirmation of Philip G. Lewis, who had been appointed Rumford's postmaster by President Eisenhower in 1959. She pointed out that Lewis had twenty-five years of honorable service in the Post Office Department behind him.

"I can only conclude that his confirmation was blocked solely by sheer partisan politics," she said. "I am proud to say I have never opposed a postal nomination made by a Democratic President."

Muskie disclaimed any thought of playing politics. He explained his two-year hesitation by saying that others were interested in the job, and that there was no competitive examination. But Maine's two Senators remained in a state of war. In 1963, when the administration informed Senator Muskie of new submarine construction to take place at the Portsmouth Naval Yard, Margaret Smith was again up in arms. A Senator can make political capital out of his advance knowledge of such information. She accused the Kennedy administration of unfair tactics (conveniently forgetting that she had gotten an occasional break on good news during the Eisenhower administration).

The battle became a three-way affair that same year when May Craig wrote in her column that hard feeling between Senators Smith and Muskie had prevented a meeting of the Maine Congressional Delegation in 1963. Margaret Smith fired back, accusing Mrs. Craig of misrepresenting the situation "by giving the false impression that we would permit any differences of principles, policies and views to degenerate into such personal pettiness as to cause cancellation of a delegation meeting dedicated to the interest of the state of Maine and the people of Maine." Muskie, hardly anxious to tumble into an argument between two enraged ladies, confined himself to the remark that he knew of Senator Smith's "deep feelings," but that he didn't react in the same way to Mrs. Craig's report.

At five o'clock in the afternoon Margaret Smith usually returns to her office to finish her dictation and sign the letters that have been typed by her staff. She leaves the office around seven, invariably carrying under her arm a case of letters and papers which she will look over at home. Sometimes she eats in Washington, at other times she goes home to Silver Spring, where she prepares her own meal. There is always some tidying up to do around the house, though a maid comes to clean several times a week. Between eight-thirty and eleven she goes over the material she has brought with her from the office (with perhaps a half-hour out for television) and, if her work is finished, prepares for bed at eleven. Once in bed, she listens to the late news, then turns off the radio and submits herself to sleep.

Less than eight hours later Margaret Smith will be back in public life.

❦ 18 ❧

THIS, then, is the woman who cast "a very troubled vote" against the Limited Test Ban Treaty at the end of 1963. Her decision should not have surprised anyone who had followed her career. Almost from girlhood, Margaret Smith has been in public life. Her experience as a public servant accounts for her curious, and sometimes contradictory, attitudes on the issues of peace and war.

As a woman, Margaret Smith must at least have momentarily welcomed the treaty. Perhaps, as President Kennedy had said, it "carried the hopes of the world." Perhaps, finally, there was a way out of the insane spiral of the building and testing of nuclear weapons . . . out of the radioactive clouds that had blighted the earth's atmosphere . . . out of the almost unbearable Cold War tensions. Margaret Smith has recognized the profound desire of the American people for peace, and of the initiative the people can take in establishing that peace.

"Peace will stem from the will of the people themselves rather than the genius of their leaders," she said in a speech some years ago. "Women can play a tremendous role by being alert and responsible citizens."

Yet against these hopes of a compassionate woman is her long experience as a legislator.

"It was my privilege and responsibility back in 1953 and 1954," she has said, "to be the chairman of the Senate Preparedness Investigating Subcommittee that investigated the ammunition shortage in the Korean war. What we found in that shocking story made a very deep and lasting impression on me. I do not want to see that tragic condition repeated."

Ten years later she read the contents of the Limited Test Ban Treaty, passed them through her mind, and produced a negative vote. How can a woman cast a vote against peace? many Americans wanted to know. One of her admirers once remarked that although she is extremely feminine and is always aware of the physical picture she presents to the public, Margaret Smith thinks like a man. She understands armaments, and the nature of power, as have few women of our time.

It has been said that many women have had political influence, but few have had political responsibility. Margaret Smith, who has that responsibility, deals in power. She might not have been effective had she gone into social work, or nursing, or fashion designing, as she was not effective when she went into teaching. She renders services to her constituents, but performs these services through power.

Always close to our armed forces, she watches world affairs more with the eyes of a general than with those of a diplomat. America's security preoccupies her. Peace, she believes, will be maintained through power (ours), because the Communists can never be trusted. In the Senate her role is with the military rather than with the pacifists, with the "hawks" rather than with the "doves." One cannot imagine Margaret Smith walking beside the mothers in a "ban-the-bomb" demonstration.

Yet, all efforts to pigeonhole her fail. Because one is not surprised at a particular decision of hers does not mean that all of her decisions can be accurately forecast. She wears the

Republican seal of approval, but she will cast it off just as quickly (and just as unpredictably) as she will that of the Air Force brass or a Maine industrialist.

A critic, upset by one of Margaret Smith's decisions during a campaign, once grumbled to a friend: "She ought to be thinking about her re-election."

And his friend replied: "Margaret doesn't have to think about elections. She thinks about people."

There is the key to her political success. She is one of the last of a great breed of Americans in public life, devoted above all to the security and welfare of her constituents, suspicious of those she feels are their enemies, and insistent on their right to their traditional independence. She is not ashamed to be called a militant patriot. Characteristically, her patriotism implies unending vigilance against those who would destroy America, and not, as is the case with so many contemporary self-styled patriots, the destruction of Americans who hold unpopular beliefs.

Less than two months after Margaret Smith had fought his Limited Test Ban Treaty in the Senate, President John F. Kennedy lay dead of an assassin's bullet. Though opposed to some of his solutions for America's problems, she had supported his call to work for a strong, prosperous country. Republicans and Democrats alike now mourned his death. On Monday, November 25, all of Washington followed the body of the young President to Arlington Cemetery. The next morning, as the Senate convened to get on once more with the business of running the country, Margaret Smith paid her own tribute to his memory. Crossing the aisle to the Democratic side of the Senate floor, she stopped at the desk where he had sat only a few years before as the junior senator from Massachusetts. Then she turned around and walked away.

Behind her, on John Kennedy's old desk, lay the fresh red rose Margaret Smith had worn on her dress a moment before.

APPENDIX

Margaret Chase Smith's
"Declaration of Conscience"
United States Senate—June 1, 1950

MR. PRESIDENT:

I would like to speak briefly and simply about a serious national condition. It is a national feeling of fear and frustration that could result in national suicide and the end of everything that we Americans hold dear. It is a condition that comes from the lack of effective leadership in either the Legislative Branch or the Executive Branch of our Government.

That leadership is so lacking that serious and responsible proposals are being made that national advisory commissions be appointed to provide such critically needed leadership.

I speak as briefly as possible because too much harm has already been done with irresponsible words of bitterness and selfish political opportunism. I speak as simply as possible because the issue is too great to be obscured by eloquence. I speak simply and briefly in the hope that my words will be taken to heart.

I speak as a Republican. I speak as a woman. I speak as a United States Senator. I speak as an American.

The United States Senate has long enjoyed worldwide respect as the greatest deliberative body in the world. But recently that deliberative character has too often been debased to the level of a forum of hate and character assassination sheltered by the shield of congressional immunity.

It is ironical that we Senators can in debate in the Senate, directly or indirectly, by any form of words impute to any American, who is not a Senator, any conduct or motive unworthy or unbecoming an American—and without that non-Senator American having any legal redress against us—yet if we say the same thing in the Senate about our colleagues we can be stopped on the grounds of being out of order.

It is strange that we can verbally attack anyone else without restraint and with full protection and yet we hold ourselves above the same type of criticism here on the Senate Floor. Surely the United States Senate is big enough to take self-criticism and self-appraisal. Surely we should be able to take the same kind of character attacks that we "dish out" to outsiders.

I think that it is high time for the United States Senate and its members to do some soul searching—for us to weigh our consciences—on the manner in which we are performing our duty to the people of America—on the manner in which we are using or abusing our individual powers and privileges.

I think that it is high time that we remembered that we have sworn to uphold and defend the Constitution. I think that it is high time that we remembered that the Constitution, as amended, speaks not only of the freedom of speech but also of trial by jury instead of trial by accusation.

Whether it be a criminal prosecution in court or a character prosecution in the Senate, there is little practical distinction when the life of a person has been ruined.

Those of us who shout the loudest about Americanism in making character assassinations are all too frequently those who, by our own words and acts, ignore some of the basic principles of Americanism—

The right to criticize;

The right to hold unpopular beliefs;

The right to protest;

The right of independent thought.

The exercise of these rights should not cost one single American citizen his reputation or his right to a livelihood nor should he be in danger of losing his reputation or livelihood merely because he happens to know some one who holds unpopular beliefs. Who of us doesn't? Otherwise none of us could call our souls our own. Otherwise thought control would have set in.

The American people are sick and tired of being afraid to speak their minds lest they be politically smeared as "Communists" or "Fascists" by their opponents. Freedom of speech is not what it used to be in America. It has been so abused by some that it is not exercised by others.

The American people are sick and tired of seeing innocent people smeared and guilty people whitewashed. But there have been enough proved cases to cause nationwide distrust and strong suspicion that there may be something to the unproved, sensational accusations.

As a Republican, I say to my colleagues on this side of the aisle that the Republican Party faces a challenge today that is not unlike the challenge that it faced back in Lincoln's day. The Republican Party so successfully met that challenge that it emerged from the Civil War as the champion of a united nation—in addition to being a Party that unrelentingly fought loose spending and loose programs.

Today our country is being psychologically divided by the confusion and the suspicions that are bred in the United

States Senate to spread like cancerous tentacles of "know nothing, suspect everything" attitudes. Today we have a Democratic Administration that has developed a mania for loose spending and loose programs. History is repeating itself —and the Republican Party again has the opportunity to emerge as the champion of unity and prudence.

The record of the present Democratic Administration has provided us with sufficient campaign issues without the necessity of resorting to political smears. America is rapidly losing its position as leader of the world simply because the Democratic Administration has pitifully failed to provide effective leadership.

The Democratic Administration has completely confused the American people by its daily contradictory grave warnings and optimistic assurances—that show the people that our Democratic Administration has no idea of where it is going.

The Democratic Administration has greatly lost the confidence of the American people by its complacency to the threat of communism here at home and the leak of vital secrets to Russia through key officials of the Democratic Administration. There are enough proved cases to make this point without diluting our criticism with unproved charges.

Surely these are sufficient reasons to make it clear to the American people that it is time for a change and that a Republican victory is necessary to the security of this country. Surely it is clear that this nation will continue to suffer as long as it is governed by the present ineffective Democratic Administration.

Yet to displace it with a Republican regime embracing a philosophy that lacks political integrity or intellectual honesty would prove equally disastrous to this nation. The nation sorely needs a Republican victory. But I don't want to see the Republican Party ride to political victory on the Four Horsemen of Calumny— Fear, Ignorance, Bigotry and Smear.

I doubt if the Republican Party could—simply because I don't believe the American people will uphold any political party that puts political exploitation above national interest. Surely we Republicans aren't that desperate for victory.

I don't want to see the Republican Party win that way. While it might be a fleeting victory for the Republican Party, it would be a more lasting defeat for the American people. Surely it would ultimately be suicide for the Republican Party and the two-party system that has protected our American liberties from the dictatorship of a one-party system.

As members of the Minority Party, we do not have the primary authority to formulate the policy of our Government. But we do have the responsibility of rendering constructive criticism, of clarifying issues, of allaying fears by acting as responsible citizens.

As a woman, I wonder how the mothers, wives, sisters and daughters feel about the way in which members of their families have been politically mangled in Senate debate— and I used the word "debate" advisedly.

As a United States Senator, I am not proud of the way in which the Senate has been made a publicity platform for irresponsible sensationalism. I am not proud of the reckless abandon in which unproved charges have been hurled from this side of the aisle. I am not proud of the obviously staged, undignified countercharges that have been attempted in retaliation from the other side of the aisle.

I don't like the way the Senate has been made a rendezvous for vilification, for selfish political gain at the sacrifice of individual reputations and national unity. I am not proud of the way we smear outsiders from the Floor of the Senate and hide behind the cloak of congressional immunity and still place ourselves beyond criticism on the Floor of the Senate.

As an American, I am shocked at the way Republicans and

Democrats alike are playing directly into the Communist design of "confuse, divide and conquer." As an American, I don't want a Democratic Administration "white wash" or "cover up" any more than I want a Republican smear or witch hunt.

As an American, I condemn a Republican "Fascist" just as much as I condemn a Democrat "Communist." I condemn a Democrat "Fascist" just as much as I condemn a Republican "Communist." They are equally dangerous to you and me and to our country. As an American, I want to see our nation recapture the strength and unity it once had when we fought the enemy instead of ourselves.

It is with these thoughts that I have drafted what I call a "Declaration of Conscience." I am gratified that Senator Tobey, Senator Aiken, Senator Morse, Senator Ives, Senator Thye and Senator Hendrickson have concurred in that declaration and have authorized me to announce their concurrence.

(The following was placed in the Congressional Record with the "Declaration of Conscience.")

STATEMENT OF SEVEN REPUBLICAN SENATORS

1. We are Republicans. But we are Americans first. It is as Americans that we express our concern with the growing confusion that threatens the security and stability of our country. Democrats and Republicans alike have contributed to that confusion.

2. The Democratic Administration has initially created the confusion by its lack of effective leadership, by its contradictory grave warnings and optimistic assurances, by its complacency to the threat of communism here at home, by its oversensitiveness to rightful criticism, by its petty bitterness against its critics.

3. Certain elements of the Republican Party have materially added to this confusion in the hopes of riding the Republican Party to victory through the selfish political exploitation of fear, bigotry, ignorance and intolerance. There are enough mistakes of the Democrats for Republicans to criticize constructively without resorting to political smears.

4. To this extent, Democrats and Republicans alike have unwittingly, but undeniably, played directly into the Communist design of "confuse, divide and conquer."

5. It is high time that we stopped thinking politically as Republicans and Democrats about elections and started thinking patriotically as Americans about national security based on individual freedom. It is high time that we all stopped being tools and victims of totalitarian techniques— techniques that, if continued here unchecked, will surely end what we have come to cherish as the American way of life.

MARGARET CHASE SMITH, *Maine*
CHARLES W. TOBEY, *New Hampshire*
GEORGE D. AIKEN, *Vermont*
WAYNE L. MORSE, *Oregon*
IRVING M. IVES, *New York*
EDWARD J. THYE, *Minnesota*
ROBERT C. HENDRICKSON, *New Jersey*

INDEX